Finding a striking or nostalgic piece of fabric can often influence or catalyze an artist's design process. From vintage clothing to antique quilts, the look and feel of a piece of fabric carries its own history and inspiration. In this book, Mandy Pattullo shows you how to repurpose materials to create beautiful and texturally interesting collages.

Before a piece of textile art can be stitched, fabrics must be sourced. Beginning with 'Materials', Mandy Pattullo guides you on how and where to find fascinating fabrics, and what to look out for. From the internet to charity shops and even your own wardrobe, inspiration can be found anywhere.

The book then progresses from a guide on how to store and dye materials to how to select and arrange various textiles to create your own collages, both abstract and representational. As well as constructing your artwork, Mandy Pattullo shows you how to add extra interest to your work with subtle stitches, appliqué, patchwork or other mediums. Then follows a feature chapter on how to compose captivating collages that take inspiration from the natural world, and how to create evocative portraits.

Moving onto 'Worn', this book demonstrates how to sew wearable art using upcycled textiles, heavily drawing upon the 'make do and mend' culture of the past. Finally, 'Book' teaches you how to create your own textile art sketchbooks and how to manipulate the fabric to weave narratives. The potential for reusing fabrics is limitless, and this book helps you to re-examine the textiles around you and see them in a new light.

To Margaret
Happy Stitching!
Best wishes
Mandy Pattullo

Textile Collage

Textile Collage

Using collage techniques in textile art

by Mandy Pattullo

BATSFORD

To Andrew

This edition was first published in the United Kingdom in 2016 by Batsford
1 Gower Street
London
WC1E 6HD

An imprint of Pavilion Books Company Limited

Copyright © Batsford, 2016
Text and illustrations © Mandy Pattullo, 2016

Unless otherwise stated, all drawings, diagrams and stitched textiles are by Mandy Pattullo.

The moral rights of the author have been asserted.

All rights reserved. No part of this publication may be reproduced, stored in a retrieval system, or transmitted in any form or by any means electronic, mechanical, photocopying, recording or otherwise, without the prior written permission of the copyright owner.

ISBN: 9781849943741

A CIP catalogue record is available from the British Library.

20 19 18 17 16
10 9 8 7 6 5 4 3 2 1

Reproduction by Mission Productions, Hong Kong.
Printed and bound by 1010 Printing International Ltd, China.

This book can be ordered direct from the publisher at: www.pavilionbooks.com, or try your local bookshop.

Distributed in the United States and Canada by Sterling Publishing Co., Inc. 1166 Avenue of the Americas, 17th floor, New York, NY 10036, USA

RIGHT: *Harmonising Hexagons*, 2014. 15 x 22cm (6 x 9in).

OPPOSITE: Flower corsage constructed from old quilt pieces and fabrics (see page 102).

Contents

Introduction 6

MATERIALS 8

Hunting and gathering 10
Fabric archaeology 21
Dyeing 22
Making marks 23
Storage and care 25

MAKE 26

Colour 28
Composition 32
Putting it together 34
Stitches 36
Finishing off 39
Changing the scale 42
Appliqué 47
Patchwork 51
Mixing paper and cloth 52

PORTRAY 56

Enchanted forest 58
Building up your collage 62
Line 65
Animal magic 67
Birds 68
People portraits 71

WORN 80

What to use 82
Getting started 84
Jackets 86
Quilt garments 90
Domestic embroidery 96
Flower corsage 102
Going small 103

BOOK 104

Things to consider 106
Quilt books 111
Scroll books 112
Making a fabric concertina book 113
Wonders with wallets 115
Collections and cloth books 119

Conclusion 124
Artists' websites and suppliers 125
Further reading 126
Index 127
Picture credits and acknowledgements 128

Introduction

I came to textile collage through a lifetime of collecting fabrics, making patchworks and training as a surface pattern designer. My training encouraged me to look at textile archives and decorative art for imagery and pattern to use in fabric design but I was also drawn to the textures and resonance of old fabrics themselves, and became a collector of antique and ethnic textiles and particularly of old quilts. There came a point where I had to start using these precious finds in my practice rather than hoarding them. By cutting, tearing and unpicking, I discovered that I was interested in mixing things up, the possibilities of layering and assembling, and found myself doing collage with fabric.

Collage is traditionally associated with paper. My favourite fine artist has always been Robert Rauschenberg, and he and Kurt Schwitters, Peter Blake and Joseph Cornell have created respected works of art through their careful arrangements of paper scraps and sometimes fabric.

The technique can easily be transferred to fabric and is a most satisfying medium in which to work because when you complete a project a transformation has occurred. From a seemingly random collection of scraps you have created a cohesive and pleasing composition. I have also chosen it as the main focus of my work because of its relationship to the thrift and

'When I adjust materials of different kinds to one another, I have taken a step in advance of mere oil painting, for in addition to playing off colour against colour, line against line, and form against form, I play off material against material…'
KURT SCHWITTERS

ABOVE: Stitching into a piece of an old log cabin quilt.

RIGHT: A corner of my studio at The Hearth, Horsley, Northumberland.

'make, do and mend' culture of past times, in particular utility patchworks and quilts made by women in domestic settings. The collages I make, like those early patchworks, bring together precious fragments to form evocative compositions. The viewer is forced to re-examine fabrics that have become flawed through wear and tear, to find in them a new beauty. My collages are nearly all hand pieced for the same reason, as the slowness of hand stitching gives me time to build up a relationship with even the shabbiest of fabrics.

Fabric collage is a kind of patchwork but without having to follow a pattern and a kind of appliqué without the templates. There is a freedom in the art of fabric collage, which allows you continually to arrange and rearrange and create anything from pictures and wall hangings to books, garments and accessories. I have done all of these things and now hope to inspire you too, to use those collections of fabric and textile treasures you have collected for years or are about to find, to indulge in fabric collage.

MATERIALS

Every artist needs materials to create a work of art. The materials may not be unusual but it is the way they use them that matters. The artist needs to develop a style and visual language where the materials are used to construct the work, but where a transformative process has been undertaken. My materials are fabric and thread – easily accessible to everyone – but I am selective about the fabrics I work with, as I want them to tell a story which is mine and not someone else's. I have chosen to work with materials that come to me not through purchasing in shops, online or at shows, but are inherited, gifted and given, or purchased second hand. I actively seek out the worn and torn. Fabrics that are stained are not rejected as they have a history, and signs of wear and tear show me that materials have been used or loved. My collection of fabrics not only gives me a palette of colours but also provide me with sensory stimulation with their rough edges, textures and stitched marks. The materials you collect need to be personal to you, and if you seek out the unusual and fabrics that are a little more difficult to find then you too will be able to develop a signature style.

LEFT: *Button Flower* (detail), 2013. 25 x 43cm (10 x 17in).

MATERIALS

Hunting and gathering

The lovely thing about fabric collage is that you have the opportunity to create a resolved piece of work using a wide variety of materials. It encourages you to collect and take a fresh look at the worn and shabby, the textured, the printed, the shiny, the transparent, the embroidered. You will not reject the stained and darned or fabrics marked by mildew and rusty pins, as all of these can be added to the mix. It is a thrill to find these items through online auction sites, visiting vintage fairs and flea markets or rummaging in charity shops. You may be lucky enough to have inherited some fabrics and embroidered pieces that hold memories for you of the person who made them. What are you keeping them for? If you are not using them, and they are stored somewhere you cannot see them, cut them up and use them to create works of art, which bring together your own hands and those of past generations. To me this link with the past is one of the most important elements of why I do what I do. As I reinvigorate, rescue and reclaim fabrics and domestic needlework from anonymous wearers and embroiderers I feel a real sense of connection to the people who wore and made them.

In this chapter I will introduce you to the interesting fabrics you can look out for and give a little bit of history about some of them. Some of the textiles described will be more suitable for the base or foundation of your piece whilst others can be cut or torn into smaller pieces for collage and appliqué.

LEFT: A fabric selection from my studio including pieces of quilt, flour sack, printed cotton, denim and furnishing fabrics.

LEFT: A pile of old patchwork quilts ready to be used as the foundations for collage or unpicked for their fabrics.

Quilts

The patchwork quilt arose from necessity. The thick wadding in between a top and bottom layer of fabric, held together by knotting or quilting stitches, provided an essential warm layer at night in the days before central heating. Quilts were sometimes carefully designed, and new and co-ordinated fabrics were bought, but on the whole the quilts of the late nineteenth and early twentieth centuries were thrifty affairs made from leftover dressmaking fabrics, recycled clothing and tailors' samples. Old patchwork quilts are my passion. I love to see how they are put together, which designs have been used and how the colours of the fabrics work next to each other. Each piece of fabric may tell a story. I particularly like those pieces that may be poor in design but incorporate bits of wool, flannel and men's shirting.

A quilt can provide both a foundation on which to work and, once unpicked, a lovely collection of old fabrics for your use.

It is becoming harder and harder to find old quilts. I look for quilts that are worn and torn; sometimes they have stains and the wadding layer is trying to escape. These ragged quilts are usually cheaper to buy as they often have areas of very fragile fabrics, which have disintegrated due to the original dyeing, printing or bleaching process. I love these tattered wisps and carefully pull them out to use within my work. When I find a pile of quilts for sale I always pick them up. If the quilt is heavy then the patchwork on the top may be covering and repairing another quilt underneath. The top layer can be removed and the usually Victorian second quilt inside revealed and used. I feel no guilt at cutting up old quilts to use in my work, as when the sections are worked on and remodelled it means that many people can once again appreciate the surfaces and patterns of that quilt, not just me. I never use quilts in perfect condition in my work but ones that are really not fit for purpose, as they are too tattered to survive as bed covers.

MATERIALS

Turkey red

The scarlet colour found in many old quilts and eiderdowns is often called Turkey red. The dye originally came from the madder plant. Its use was developed in the Middle East, but by the late eighteenth century there were commercial dye companies in England and Scotland producing huge amounts of colourfast Turkey red cotton fabric for the home and export markets, and Turkey red fabric could be found across the world. Other colours and patterns were mixed in with the red, with the development of a discharge process, which could bleach away the red to reveal white. The white areas could be printed with black, blue and yellow, and green was created by overprinting blue with yellow. By the twentieth century a synthetic dye was developed and the use of the plant-based dye declined.

Turkey red fabrics in Britain were used for dresses and also for down-filled petticoats, eiderdowns and quilts. The use of Turkey red within quilt design was at its height in the late nineteenth and early twentieth century. When red was combined with white it produced dramatic quilts such as the quilted 'strippy' from the North East of England or appliquéd and log cabin designs imported from the United States.

The best source of authentic printed Turkey red fabric for collage is the eiderdown. These often have a thick layer of cotton wadding inserted for warmth. The thickness makes them difficult to collage on to or use because of the lumpiness but the pretty printed fabrics can be unpicked and the wadding discarded. These old fabrics can be extremely delicate so will not withstand repeated washing after they have been applied.

RIGHT: *Turkey Red*, 2014. 45 x 45cm (18 x 18in). A cushion cover using a variety of Turkey red eiderdown fabrics.

MATERIALS

Curtain fabrics and linings

There is no shortage of new curtain fabric to buy but look in auctions and charity shops for old curtain fabric with beautiful patterns and designs, whether it be 1950s retro, figurative toile de Jouy or Arts & Crafts prints. Faded florals, crumpled chintz and retro prints are all collectable and when used within a collage might provide the start of a colour story or the pattern might suggest stitch schemes. I particularly like old linen printed fabric that may have been unevenly bleached out by the sun. Curtain linings that have maybe touched a damp window and show signs of foxing or mildew immediately provide an 'aged' appeal.

Bump curtain lining, a lining fabric which has wadding bonded onto it, is useful as a foundation fabric or backing for fabric collage.

Upholstery fabrics such as cut or devoré velvet, woven tapestry, brocades, damasks and silks can be used. I have even incorporated some of my grandmother's old sofa fabric in some of my work. Your work will immediately have more integrity if some of the ingredients have a link with your own life story.

Printed fabrics

I prefer to use old rather than buy new, and cottons and linens rather than synthetic fabrics. When clothes are discarded in our household they are sorted into a pile for the charity shop and a pile to be cut up. Men's shirts, printed cotton skirts and blouses are cut up for the fabrics and buttons. Don't discard cuffs or front fastenings as these details might be used somewhere. Look for second-hand garments that can be recycled into your work.

I only use pure cotton fabric for finger-turned appliqué in a project. Cotton holds a crease when you press it with a finger or iron, which make it ideal for turned edges. Fortunately, beautiful cotton patchwork fabrics can now be easily obtained from specialized shops. The designs are sometimes reproduced from historic sources so it is easy to match the style of old patchwork quilts. I don't buy much new fabric but every now and then will buy a fat quarter of fabric if I am running short of colours. I nearly always use the back of these newer crisp printed fabrics or tea dye them or use them within a border. Floral prints such as those from Liberty are great to cut up to extract tiny individual flowers for appliqué details and I love French General's prints, inspired by French archive research.

LEFT: *Peony*, 2015. 34 x 23cm (13 x 9in). Pieces of old and stained curtain fabrics provide a patchwork base for the appliquéd needlepoint peony.

MATERIALS

Blue

ABOVE: *Spotted Star*, 2013. 41 x 27cm (16 x 10½in). A piece inspired by boro textiles but using over-dyed British quilt fragments.

BELOW: *A is for Andrew*, 2014. 16 x 22cm (6 x 9in). A teaching sample mixing recycled denim with an old cross-stitch tablecloth.

When you think of blue cloth you might almost immediately picture denim. Denim is a robust fabric associated with blue jeans. The first jeans were worn during the Californian gold rush and are now 'mined' in the same way as gold was because even tiny scraps of original Levi Strauss workwear are highly collectable. Indigo-dyed jeans may fade with washing and will become distressed with repeated wearing. This is when denim becomes so much more interesting. If you cut up a pair of jeans you will have a palette of blue fabrics with various degrees of staining, and unpicking seams will reveal the original blue. There is, of course, the detailing too – pockets, rivets, labels and the iconic orange stitching of the original designs. Using a little bit of denim in a collage will have resonance with almost everyone.

The quilt makers of Gee's Bend, a once isolated community in Alabama, utilized denim within their quilt-making out of necessity. They transformed the worn-out jeans of their menfolk into dynamic bed quilts which have now been re-appropriated by the fine art world and hang in major North American museums. This redefining of craft into art has also happened with Japanese 'boro' textiles. Boro means 'tattered rags' in Japanese and refers to the tradition of patching and repairing humble materials, particularly indigo-dyed fabric, so that they may continue to be used in times of economic necessity. We now revere these textiles produced in poverty for their naïve patchwork compositions, the surface qualities of the worn fabrics and the stitching used to hold them all together. We can learn a lot from a close examination of the way they instinctively layered and collaged together scraps.

It is unlikely that you will be able to get hold of an original piece of boro textile to use within your work but you might be able to source old kimonos or more contemporary Japanese indigo-dyed fabrics. If you really like the look then you might be able to re-create it through indigo dyeing very distressed old fabrics such as worn quilt tops, as I sometimes do.

ABOVE: *Pink Flower*, 2015. 14½ x 20cm (6 x 8in). The back of an Indian embroidery mixed in with linsey-woolsey cloth, a flower from a cushion cover and pieces of quilt.

Lace

There are so many different types of lace – crochet, bobbin lace, net lace and tatting. Examples can easily be found in thrift or charity shops or you can cut lace off garments or old linen. Most old lace is made from cotton so it dyes well. I avoid using too much lace, particularly as a trim, as it can be a distraction and 'prettify' a piece of work. When I use it I cut sections out of it, shredded or torn, so it looks less contrived.

Found embroidery

I sometimes like to incorporate pieces of stitching that have been done by someone in the past or from another culture. I look for embroidered napkins, handkerchiefs, tablecloths and runners in charity shops and flea markets. These are usually cheap because they are no longer valued. Monograms and name labels were often used to distinguish the ownership of pieces sent to a laundry and can be cut off and used to add text in a piece. I will pay more for exquisite historical pieces or stitched work from other cultures. These can be purchased online but I prefer to find them at vintage and antique textile fairs so that I can handle the pieces and see their true colours and quality. Exquisite examples of historic embroidery from China, Japan and India can be used in textile collages and can add a real focus to a piece, like a precious jewel. Indian embroidered goods are easy to find; they can sometimes be crude but always check the back of the embroidery as this is occasionally more interesting.

Silks

Silk has a softness and transparency that is unique. It was often used in Victorian log cabin quilts and has a tendency to disintegrate with time. You might find an old silk petticoat or dress which is too thin and worn to work with but can be torn up and dyed. Look for old silk scarves and Indian printed silk garments second hand. **Debra Weiss** uses scraps of silks in her collages. She explains her reason:

'They started as a "controlled chaos" series. As the recession progressed in 2008 I had to make many changes in my business and gathered eight years of scraps of silks once used for bags and stopped that part of my business. I sorted and collaged and stitched the pieces as organically as they were left. I employed the transparency of many of the pieces to resemble our lives, the years and years of growth and experience making us who we are. The stitching flattening it all to the soul of ourselves.'

RIGHT: Debra Weiss. *Layers of a Life*, 2008. 71 x 46cm (28 x 18in). Silk scraps collaged and stitched with running stitch.

Tweeds and tailors' samples

Beautiful tweeds such as Harris Tweed are always going to be expensive. Think outside the box and look for tweed skirts and jackets in car boot sales and charity shops. If you are really lucky you might be able to get a hold of a quilt made from tweeds and wool. These were usually made from tailors' samples. Check for moth damage or any sign that they might still be active in this wool fabric that they particularly love.

RIGHT: *Button Flower*, 2013. 25 x 43cm (10 x 17in). A piece of needlepoint supplied the colour theme for this piece, which utilizes old tailors' samples.

MATERIALS

Needlepoint

The use of needlepoint or petit point within textile collage has become a signature style of my work. Needlepoint is worked in tapestry wool onto canvas, usually onto a printed-design canvas, which is provided in kit form with all the wool you need to complete the project. Many hours of labour go into making a tapestry cushion so it is quite common to find unfinished projects. I am especially interested in the back of tapestry where the design is obscured by threads crossing and knots. I do not worry about cutting into needlepoint and through the stitches as my collages are designed to be hung on the wall and are not going to be laundered or heavily used. Petit point is especially lovely because it is constructed using very small, fine stitches. A finished needlepoint is quite a robust textile and can be upcycled into bags or used on garments.

Blankets

Wool blankets are a very good substitute for an old quilt as a foundation fabric for collage. Before duvets they were commonly used on beds and can be sourced easily and over-dyed if you wish with natural and acid dyes. If you are cutting a blanket up make sure you keep the label and the satin or blanket-stitched edge. It is a really special moment when you find a lovely darned section on a blanket. This indicates that the blanket has been valued and mended rather than thrown out and replaced. I love to mix them up with needlepoint also worked in wool.

RIGHT: *Signs of Autumn*, 2015. 26 x 24cm (10 x 9½in). Detail of collage showing the use of needlepoint, blanket and tweed.

MATERIALS

Flour and feed sacks

When times were hard women sought fabric wherever they could to use in their quilts. In the nineteenth and early twentieth century cotton sacking was used by manufacturers to store and transport dry goods. Seed and flour sacks would regularly come into homes and the thrifty lady of the house would keep the sacks, launder them and recycle them. They can sometimes be found on the backs of early twentieth-century patchwork and in the United States feed sacks were used for clothing too. In fact the manufacturers began to trade on this and started to print the feed sacks with patterns that could be used specifically for dressmaking.

In my area of the north of England a big flour mill was established at Silloth on the Solway Estuary in 1887. It later became Carr's and flour sacks can sometimes be sourced at antique fairs locally or found incorporated into the backing of quilts. When I can get hold of them I love to use them within a fabric collage because it is a way of bringing in some lettering and relating my work to a locality. The bags are usually very fine and soft and best used on the top of another fabric or wadding to support them. Vintage feed sacks are quite easy to source through online auction sites though those that were used in the UK are rarer.

ABOVE: *70lbs*, 2013. 35 x 25cm (14 x 10in). A piece of a Carr's flour sack provides the focus against the dark layers of over-dyed quilt pieces.

LEFT: Wool and ribbon embroidery on a contemporary potato sack.

MATERIALS

Threads

As well as fabrics you should start to assemble a collection of threads. The sort of cotton or polycotton threads that you use in a sewing machine will be invaluable in assembling your textile collage. For your decorative stitching you will need embroidery threads, which come in a wide range of colours and thicknesses. I find stranded cottons (six stranded floss) the most useful as you can separate the strands. I tend to use two or three strands for nearly all the embroidery I do. I rarely use perlé thread as it has a slight shine, which does not always sit well with old and worn surfaces. Coton á broder, a soft cotton thread, is much more suitable. Sashiko thread is another loosely twisted cotton thread, which is often used to create dense rows of running stitch on Japanese style quilts.

You might buy old threads on wooden spools or cards but be wary of these as sometimes the quality of the thread has deteriorated with time and it has lost its strength.

ABOVE: A variety of threads including perlé, wool, coton à broder, sashiko and stranded floss.

MATERIALS

Fabric archaeology

The 'quick-unpick' or seam ripper is one of the most useful tools in the textile artist's tool kit. This tool, with its curved blade, is designed to remove small, tight stitches. It is most commonly used to 'open' buttonholes, to correct mistakes in stitching or within dressmaking to alter seams, but it is also an essential tool for unpicking old patchwork, garments, embroidery and curtains to create interesting fabrics to work with.

Thick and worn-out old patchwork quilts that are badly made or too lumpy to appliqué onto can still be useful in providing a palette of unique vintage fabrics. Functional quilts made for daily use often became torn and stained and a thrifty housewife, or the next generation, increased the longevity of the quilt's life by sewing another patchwork top over the original. A 1930s or 1940s printed patchwork top may be disguising a Victorian quilt, and an exciting strata of fabrics and textures will be revealed through some careful unpicking.

I will sometimes just remove the top layer to reveal the patchwork or worn textures underneath. This newly revealed surface might act as a foundation fabric for appliqué or collage. Sometimes I will go all the way and remove all the quilting stitches, so that the quilt falls apart and goes back to its components.

This unpicking process is slow, perhaps even slower than the original maker working to sew it together, but each stitch and piece of fabric has a resonance and story to tell, which is revealed through exploring the quilt archaeology. Gradually I will amass a pile of fragile and worn fabrics, which can be used within a collage or to patch up garments or worn areas of other textiles. Both sides of the fabrics will hold potential as exposure to sun and wear and tear will have faded the top side but all of the original colour will have been retained on the back. The shadows of needle pricking where the stitches were made and the ghost marks made by the original seam, which can be difficult to iron out, can be used as an essential component in a new piece of patching.

The same process can be applied to unpicking garments. Men's jackets in particular are a joy to unpick as they reveal the inner construction of the garment.

BELOW: A seam ripper is an essential tool for unpicking old quilts to reveal the layers of fabric within.

MATERIALS

Dyeing

Sometimes I am short of a particular colour in my palette of fabrics so I will have a dyeing day. I rarely dye in the conventional sense of dyeing a white piece of cloth a different colour but I over-dye many things to knock back a colour and to see what happens when a print is overdyed. I do not attempt to dye wool but cotton, silks and bits of quilt can all be dyed effectively. I use Dylon machine and hand-wash dyes. Always follow the instructions on the packet, particularly about the suggested weight of fabric to dye powder. If you put more fabric in then you will inevitably get a paler colour. Always protect your hands by wearing rubber gloves as dye powder is caustic.

I do not like to use any fabrics with a hint of white in them. This is a personal choice. I will tea dye to turn the white into a cream or more natural colour. To do this, pour 1 litre of boiling water over two tea bags. Allow the tea bags to steep until you have the required strength of colour. I don't leave them in for very long. Remove the tea bags and allow the solution to cool. Dip your fabric in and rotate. Let it absorb the tea for a few minutes and then hang up to dry. If you are tea dyeing thick pieces of quilt then you might find that you get an uneven stain as it dries over the thick quilted wadding.

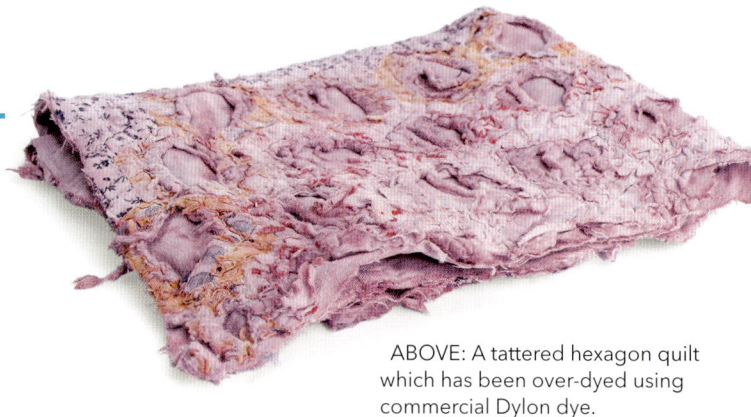

ABOVE: A tattered hexagon quilt which has been over-dyed using commercial Dylon dye.

Some artists use other methods to colour their cloth. **Claire Wellesley-Smith** creates her own range of beautiful cloth using natural dyes. She has a dye garden on her allotment and uses traditional dyers' plants in association with mordants to create soft, permanent colours. She also experiments with seasonal flowers, roots and leaves. Claire does not always dye the whole piece of fabric but dip dyes and paints too so the traces of the dye sit subtly in the folds and are washed in gradations across the cloth. This subtle range of coloured cloth, alongside her hand-dyed threads, is used within her collaged pieces, which celebrate what she calls 'slow stitch'. Her fabrics are patched together and stitched across with tiny stitches, mostly running stitches, and effectively blend the fabrics together into a resolved piece.

LEFT: Claire Wellesley-Smith. *Chase-devil Sutra*, 2014. 23 x 23cm (9 x 9in). Handstitch on wool. Threads and cloth dyed using *Hypericum perforatum* (St John's Wort, or Chase-devil) grown at Claire's allotment with iron modifier made from scrap found at the same site.

Making marks

I work with retrieved textiles and though I might unpick to reveal the punctures and seams made by a previous needle I do not alter the actual surface of the cloth. If there are any marks made on the cloth they have been made by the passage of time or are stains acting as evidence of past wear and tear. For some artists, however, putting their personal imprint on the cloth before they start to patch and collage it together is an essential part of their working process.

Matthew Harris's base cloth is cotton twill, which he transforms through the use of dyes, mark making and printing. He creates stains, blotches, brush strokes and repeated marks, which are sometimes painterly, blurred and washed out and at other times appear scratchy, heavy and dark. The greys, blacks and reds look almost rubbed or pummelled into the surface of the cloth. The cloth holds the colour and marks like bruises and scratches on the skin. The twill is a tough utilitarian fabric, which the dye will not penetrate easily, and the slow seepage through layers of folded and pleated cloth echoes his initial preparation through the production of a series of drawings or 'cartoons'. Textures, lines and washes of colour are made on papers, which are torn, folded and stitched, and are essential to the development of both the painted marks on cloth and the finished visual idea. The ease with which paper can be layered, overlapped and turned encourages the marks to be broken up and allows Harris to experiment with composition and work with the accidental, which he can in turn take into the construction of the cloth works. These share the same lively characteristics of the drawings, the cloth being torn, layered and pulled together with hand stitching, creating work where the viewer is forced to follow colour and mark that travel across the piece but which is also interrupted and displaced through the construction process.

Narita Bloom Cloth is part of a series of work responding to Matthew Harris's visits to Japan and his immersion in the aesthetic of their textiles and culture. His work chimes with the Japanese idea of wabi-sabi, which recognizes the impermanence and transient nature of things and accepts that there is beauty in the unfinished and incomplete. Harris may try to control the process of altering the cloth through the application of coloured dyes but he also celebrates the accidental traces that happen on the journey.

ABOVE: Matthew Harris. *Narita Bloom Cloth*, 2012. 170 x 99cm (67 x 39in). Dyed and printed hand-stitched cloth.

Debbie Lyddon

The collages that Debbie Lyddon makes are made up of many layers. She starts by painting up a quantity of cloth with a ground of gesso, which gives a pleasing weight and stiffness to it. She uses heavy, utilitarian fabrics such as linen and cotton duck that have a feel of tarpaulins or boat covers. Next she floats washes of acrylic or watercolour over the top, often using the cloth itself as a palette as she mixes the colours directly onto it. The colours she uses, Payne's grey, Prussian blue and yellow ochre, express for her the landscape and light of the north Norfolk coast. She cuts up these painted cloths to create a base onto which she machine stitches yet more cut forms. Sometimes wax is layered on top. The wax is either brushed lightly on to create a texture that will resist further washes of colour, or used in a heavy, thick coating that can be scratched into to create drawn lines. She finally rubs oil paint or shoe polish into the grooves in the wax to highlight the textures and to add more colour before finishing with hand-stitched loops, twists and knots.

ABOVE: Debbie Lyddon. *Marshscape Collage 11*, 2013. 33 x 27cm (13 x 11in). Cotton duck, linen, wax, metal and linen thread.

MATERIALS

Storage and care

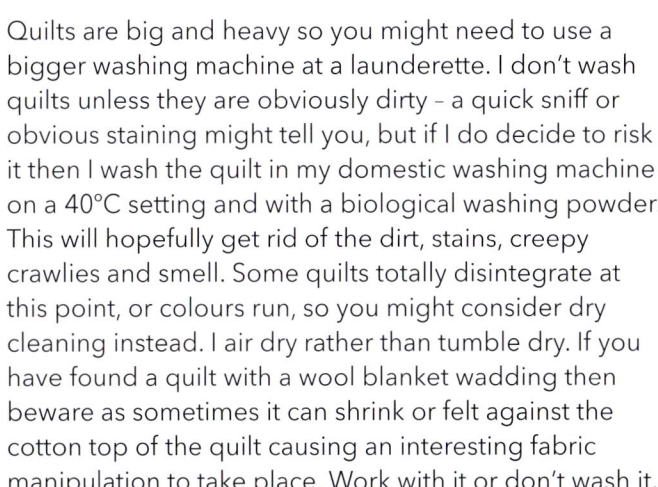

Fabrics do look lovely piled up on shelves or in baskets but beware of moths! Quilt wadding, blankets, tweeds and silk are all susceptible to infestation so I prefer to store mine in clear plastic boxes when I am not in the middle of a project. Really precious bits of old silk or embroidery are wrapped in acid-free tissue paper. Moths like dirty fabrics and because you are using a lot of old fabrics you might need to launder them before you use them. I risk most things in the washing machine but always separate into darks and lights. It can end in a disaster if all the fabrics are not colourfast but I accept whatever happens and sometimes end up with a selection of dyed fabrics rather than washed fabrics. Wools and fine lace are washed by hand in lukewarm water with soap flakes and dried flat on a towel as you would a precious cashmere sweater.

Quilts are big and heavy so you might need to use a bigger washing machine at a launderette. I don't wash quilts unless they are obviously dirty – a quick sniff or obvious staining might tell you, but if I do decide to risk it then I wash the quilt in my domestic washing machine on a 40°C setting and with a biological washing powder. This will hopefully get rid of the dirt, stains, creepy crawlies and smell. Some quilts totally disintegrate at this point, or colours run, so you might consider dry cleaning instead. I air dry rather than tumble dry. If you have found a quilt with a wool blanket wadding then beware as sometimes it can shrink or felt against the cotton top of the quilt causing an interesting fabric manipulation to take place. Work with it or don't wash it.

I don't store my materials according to type but gather them together in colour stories, for example, all the colours of autumn together, a sea and shore palette, decay and rust, opulence, brights. I iron my fabrics so they take up less space and then tie them into bundles. I have a limited amount of storage space, namely 24 under-bed plastic boxes, so once a year if carrier bags of 'extra' fabrics are cluttering up my studio then I will be ruthless and get rid of things I know that I will not use personally or cannot teach with. I always pass these on to schools, community art projects or back to charity shops. In this chapter I have encouraged you to collect and be inspired by many different types of fabrics but you can have too much!

LEFT: Mothballs will have been inserted in between the layers of these laundered quilts.

MAKE

Having collected together some of the fabrics I have suggested and maybe altered the surface through dyeing, mark making or unpicking, you are now ready to start making a fabric collage. In traditional collage paper pieces are pasted onto a support, but in fabric collage they are usually stitched onto a fabric base. It is still the same idea of bringing together individual elements and creating something that is an effective blend of colour, texture and pattern. There is an immediacy to the art of collage that allows you to respond instinctively and quickly to your fabrics and is an easy introduction to textiles because technical skills are less important. Like paper collage, pieces can overlap and be layered, edges can be torn or straight, with the raw edge visible or with edges turned under. Essentially the technique used is appliqué, which means 'applied' or 'put on'. The difference between fabric collage and appliqué is that appliqué is planned, often with templates and a design prepared, but a collage approach gives you a bit more freedom to play and be flexible because pieces can be moved easily and mistakes can be always be covered up with another layer.

LEFT: *Harmonising Hexagons* (detail), 2014. 15 x 22cm (6 x 9in).

MAKE

Colour

Once you have accumulated your collection of old and interesting fabrics how do you get started? It sounds obvious but you must be able to see your fabrics. Get them out of storage and put them on a large table. They might be in colour bundles but now mix them up a bit and allow them to unfold like flowers. If you are too organized you won't be able to find the unexpected colour combinations that are revealed through having a jumbled mess rather than tidy piles.

There are many books that offer advice about colour theory. These can be useful if you are painting or if you are using only plain coloured fabrics but when you are faced with a selection of fabrics that are printed, partially faded and have different textures you may need to abandon theory and work with the colours that excite you and which you feel confident working with. Develop palettes that are personal to you. If you have an emotional response to what you have assembled at the start of a project then it is likely that others will too. This does not mean that you should be unaware of colour altogether. I am conscious that the main impact of the finished piece might come through the use of colour and that I need to be constantly vigilant of the way a fabric can take on a different appearance, depending which colour is used next to it.

I work instinctively with the fabrics but it is sometimes helpful to have a colour story in your mind. This can be taken from a magazine tear sheet or a postcard from a museum or art gallery of a work of art. Lifestyle magazines are ideal for tearing up as a stylist has already assessed which colours work together. For example, a still life on the front of a magazine which hinges round a duck feather in the bottom of a pastel blue dish on a weathered wood table or a pile of ripe pumpkins piled up under autumnal foliage can give you the incentive to collect materials in that colour scheme. I have found the many books written by Tricia Guild, of the interior design company Designers Guild, invaluable. She has a real eye for colour but is also willing to take risks in dropping unexpected brights into a muted palette, which immediately bring vitality to a safe scheme.

I am not thinking of the composition at all at this stage but putting together colours that 'work'. My next stage is to gather these together and clip them onto a clipboard and hang them on the wall. This gives me the chance to look at them from a distance and live with them for a bit. I can add things from the pile of mixed-up fabrics and take away. I usually have several clipboards on the go so that I always have future projects to turn to and at some point I can tidy the fabrics away and get started.

It is also useful to look at the way other artists use colour and learn from them.

RIGHT: Fabrics and threads can easily be added and taken away from this clipboard until you get your colour story right. The clipboard can be hung on a wall so that you can see the colour combinations from a distance. The overlay from the central clip is already starting to suggest compositional possibilities.

MAKE

RIGHT: Anne Smith. *Neon Petunias*, 2006. 145 x 147cm (57 x 58in). Patchwork, quilting, hand and machine stitching.

Anne Smith

Anne Smith is primarily a quilt maker and uses colour with great confidence, constructing exuberant quilts and smaller work in a very limited studio space in rural Wales. She uses the quilt structure of top, bottom and middle layer stitched together as the form for her work but there is so much more going on in the layering of the top surface than in traditional patchwork and quilting. The collages she creates are intentionally painterly, full of marks and textures and, although they appear spontaneous, are actually planned through investigations in sketchbooks and painted studies, which help her to explore ideas about composition and colour before she invests the huge amount of time it takes to make the finished piece. Her work is mostly abstract and draws on the influence of the American abstract expressionist painters, particularly Rauschenberg with his collages of paint, found images, fabric and ephemera. Anne likes the strong and instant palette of colours that fabrics can provide, the use of patterned fabrics to create elements of surprise and tension and the physicality of the materials that can be manipulated in terms of surface decoration. She has built up her fabric stash through buying garments in charity shops, washing and cutting them up and sometimes retaining the essential detailing of a garment, for example the line of buttonholes or a selvedge which can creep into her work. Stitch is not just used in a functional way to pull the three layers together but is carefully considered to create a series of marks and scribbles. Sometimes these are made by working on the sewing machine from the back of the piece with unexpected results.

OPPOSITE: *Red and Green Should Never be Seen*, 2015. 28 x 21cm (11 x 8in). You might not be able to wear these colours together but the rule can be broken in textile collage where the red and green is brought together with pink and brown for an unusual colour combination.

Composition

The art of composition is a difficult one. Successful paintings marry together colour, form, contextual meaning and sometimes narrative, but in a collage the texture of the materials used plays a more predominant role in the initial impact of the piece. It is difficult to identify why some collages work and others don't, but you can learn a lot by looking at other pieces of art and working out what it is about favourite works that appeal to you. Most successful works of art have a focal point, which, in the case of fabric collage, could be one piece of special fabric around which the rest of the composition is hinged. This focal point draws the viewer in. It might be the colour that first captures your attention and it is likely that it is used in both dominant and subdominant roles. Rarely do I have a plan, particularly if it is an abstract response to the fabric itself. If the ultimate aim is something representational I will use a drawing or photograph to refer to. This process is discussed on page 60.

ABOVE: *Mustard Mix*, 2013. 38 x 27cm (15 x 10½in). The green buttonhole circles draw the eye across this collage, encouraging you to move from left to right towards the hexagon flower. The mustard-colour fabric also repeats itself effectively, bringing some unity to the piece which contains many different shapes, sizes and textures of fabric.

MAKE

Things to consider

- **The main background colour.** Is the foundation fabric going to be covered up entirely or is it going to play a lead part? If you have a large piece of fabric as a component of your collage does it need to be broken up?

- **Scale.** Your work will be uninteresting if all your fabrics are the same scale and if all the printed fabrics are using the same scale motif. A variation in the size of the pieces will make it more exciting.

- **Complexity.** Is there too much going on? I am often guilty of this. I have a pile of lovely things and want to include them all, but the individual parts need room to breathe and restful areas should be incorporated into your scheme. Spaces between can often appear empty but added interest, either in the form of tiny scraps or stitching, can resolve them at a later stage in the making process.

- **Continuity.** Do colours travel across the piece? If I am using a key colour such as red then I will bring it in in several areas, whether subtly through the use of prints with tiny hints of red within them or in pieces of fabric of various different scales (as seen on page 26).

- **Balance.** It is probably not a good idea to have all light fabrics or all dark but to have a contrast between dark and light areas. This makes the piece more lively and creates a harmony such as is present in great paintings.

- **Flexbility.** If you are getting stuck at the layout stage then just remove all your pieces and start again. The joy of a collage approach is that pieces can be continually rearranged. Sometimes turning the whole piece round from portrait to landscape will give you a new perspective.

Debra Weiss's compositions are entirely determined by the 'found' shape of the fabric pieces. As part of a project to waste nothing she began to compose with the scrap fabric collected after the production of her clothing collections. She uses each scrap of fabric just as it is, cutting nothing. She says: 'I am simply responding to the relationships between colour and form in the same way one would a painting or collage.' The series will be completed when she reaches 100 works.

LEFT: Debra Weiss. *Fabric Works No. 26, 42, 46.* 61 x 91cm (24 x 36in). Machine-stitched collage of dressmaking remnants.

33

MAKE

LEFT: Using the flying duck fabric as the key feature, different sized pieces of fabrics are placed next to and overlapping each other to try out colour combinations and compositions. Before they are pinned and sewn these pieces can constantly be rearranged until the collage works.

Putting it together

You have assembled a selection of interesting fabrics and textures to work with and decided on your colour scheme. You are now ready to put together a fabric collage. Here is how I do it:

Ingredients

- **Foundation fabric** – piece of quilt, bump curtain lining, thick blanket. Something that is strong enough to support the weight of other fabrics.
- **Collage fabrics of different weights, textures and surface interest**
- Cotton or polyester sewing threads
- Embroidery threads
- Needles, pins and scissors

Method

- Cut your foundation to the required size. Decide whether you are going to work portrait or landscape. Be flexible about this. You might find that you finish the pinning stage, turn your work round and it looks better from a different perspective.

- Cut and tear fabrics to different shapes and sizes. A one metre piece of fabric is unmanageable so make your pieces A4 or smaller. Have some really tiny pieces too. This collage method encourages you to celebrate the qualities of a torn edge and fraying so you might want to tear your fabrics rather than cut.

- Choose a key feature fabric which could be a print, a piece of needlepoint, a piece of found embroidery or a piece of old patchwork. This will probably be leading your colour scheme. Place this key component somewhere on your foundation – not in the middle or right at the edge. It can be moved later but this will get you going.

- Start to place the fabrics onto the foundation fabric and around your key piece. Make sure there are differences in scale – so some long vertical or horizontal elements, some tiny pieces which might be layered onto other fabrics. You might like to think about tone so that you have some really dark areas and other lighter. You will probably have a mix of some printed or embroidered fabrics and some plains which will provide quiet spaces. Unless you have a really interesting piece of quilt underneath which you want to keep exposed the idea is to cover the foundation with fabric until you have a pleasing composition. Make sure your fabrics overlap each other a little bit so no part of foundation peeps through.

- You must assess the work in progress and be prepared to reposition elements over and over again. If you do not pin initially you will have more of an incentive to do this. The accidental discoveries you make by continually moving elements make fabric collage much more exciting that conventional planned appliqué. This process is instinctive and there are no set rules. It is better to be really critical of your work at the initial planning stage than when you have put a lot of stitches into it!

- Pin everything onto the foundation when you are happy with the composition.

- You are now ready to stitch everything together. Use an appropriate needle and a sewing thread which is close in colour to the piece you are going to attach. Sew your fabrics onto the backing fabric with tiny stab stitches which are as unobtrusive as possible. If there is a nice fraying edge which I want to retain then I make the stab stitches just inside this edge. If the edges are not frayed then I might secure with an overstitch that actually goes over the edge of the applied fabric onto the foundation.

- You may prefer less discreet stitches to attach the fabrics to the base and there is nothing stopping you using thick embroidery threads and decorative stitches such as herringbone or buttonhole to secure your pieces.

- Enjoy the process of slow stitching and remember that you can easily move things around or add more fabrics as you are sewing. Once everything is secure remove the pins.

ABOVE: Use tiny stab stitches or overstitches to attach your fabrics to the foundation.

Things to Consider

- Do not work too big to start with. Most of my collages are A4 size or slightly larger.

- Use a camera to take pictures of your initial arrangement on the base fabric. If you move pieces around you can return to this for reference.

- Take a break or leave your work out overnight before you start to sew it together. When you return to your work any problem areas will be obvious and you can start to reposition with a fresh perspective.

- Use the correct needle for the job. You will be using a thin general-purpose cotton or polyester thread to attach your pieces so use a fine needle, a 'sharp' or a specialist appliqué needle.

- If you do not have the patience to hand stitch your collage together then use a sewing machine to attach the pieces to the foundation. Be aware, however, that this will create a hard line over those lovely soft frayed edges.

MAKE

Stitches

Embroidery stitches will add accents of colour, texture and surface decoration to your collage. Think of them like words; they can be sewn in a continuing line like a long sentence, but become more interesting if you put in breathing spaces like commas or make some stitches bolder or to act like an exclamation mark. They can also be used to blend your whole collage together, crossing the edges and into the next fabric. I sometimes try to make my stitches look like they have been thrown onto the top of the fabric like grains of rice. They should be seen as a mark-making tool and, once learnt, can be manipulated and stretched and tried in different threads, fine ribbons or cords.

Your choice of stitches might be determined by a print pattern within the work that suggests the shape of a stitch; for example many Victorian fabrics were printed with little twiggy sprigs that can be replicated in a fine fern stitch. Striped fabrics give natural lines to sew in between or on to. The use of a spotty fabric might be linked to an area of French knots somewhere else in the piece. Stitches can be used in areas where there is perhaps nothing going on, or they can be used massed together with tiny bits of collage to make the viewer focus on one area. I don't put too many stitches on my collages as it is the blocked collage of fabrics itself that is more important to me.

LEFT: Star stitches in bright red add highlights to a dark textile collage.

ABOVE: *Sprig*, 2014. 32 x 22cm (12½ x 9in). The delicate white stitching which trails across this piece has been suggested by the fern print in the top left-hand corner.

MAKE

Favourite stitches

These are personal favourites. I am a great advocate of knowing just a few stitches and doing them well. Make a sample book or create little stitch samples that inspire you on to a range of the sort of interesting fabrics you might use in a collage. You can use these as a guide when it comes to stitch.

STRAIGHT/FLAT STITCHES
Running stitch
Backstitch
Seeding or dot stitch
Satin stitch
Long and short stitch
Cross stitch
Couching
Stem stitch
Fern stitch

CHAINED STITCHES
Chain stitch
Detached chain stitch
Wheatear stitch
Lazy daisy

KNOTTED STITCHES
French knot
Bullion knot

LOOPED STITCHES
Buttonhole
Cretan
Feather
Fly

CROSSED STITCHES
Cross stitch
Herringbone
Thorn stitch
Double cross

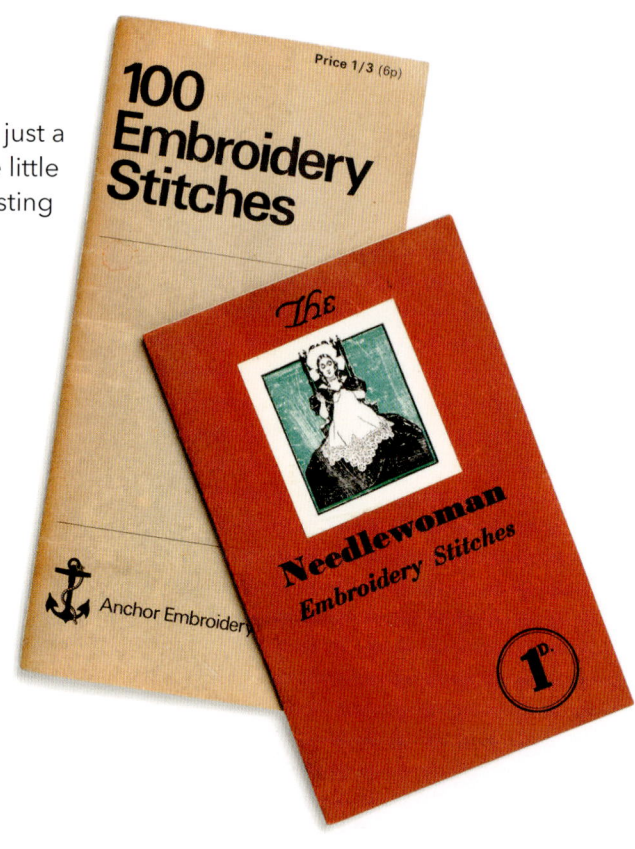

BELOW: Embroidery stitch samples on a variety of base fabrics including buttonhole, satin, feather, eyelet, wheatear, thorn stitch and French knots.

Finishing off

When your collage is finished it will need pressing. Press initially from the wrong side with the iron on a medium setting and then turn over and iron the front through a layer of non-stick baking paper. If you are confident that all the fabrics you have used are natural fibres you could increase the heat setting a bit.

Your completed fabric collage can be hung, mounted and finished off in a variety of ways depending on personal taste. The main decision you will need to make is whether to mount and frame or whether you prefer to allow the textile to be unglazed and simply hung on the wall in the style of a small wall hanging. The other consideration is whether to keep the raw edges or neaten them up.

I like to do a combination of both for most of my pieces, by placing a backing on and then bringing an edge round to neaten it up. Here's how:

Ingredients

- **Cotton backing fabric** – which complements the colours within your collage. Don't exclude printed fabrics.
- **Pins, needle and thread**

Method

- Cut your backing fabric to 5cm (2in) larger than the collage.

- Pin the collage onto the backing fabric with the 'wrong' side of the backing fabric facing upwards.

- Fold and tuck the edge of the backing fabric *underneath* the collage and pin in place. You are aiming for just a tiny amount of backing to peep through all round the edge. It will provide a straight edge while also retaining the frayed edges of the collage.

- Sew the edges of the collage onto the backing fabric using a tiny overstitch. Match the colour of the thread to the edge fabrics of the collage so it is almost invisible.

An alternative way of finishing off would be to bring the backing fabric over the top of the collage, fold and hem into place.

If you want your collage to hang freely with its fraying edges then simply stitch a piece of felt onto the back, which will cover all the mess.

To hang the collage sew curtain rings onto the top corners of the piece, which will allow it to hang on nails.

ABOVE: *Indian Flowers*, 2015. 30 x 23cm (12 x 9in). The black backing fabric is tucked under the collage and sewn into place so it just peeps out unevenly around the edges.

MAKE

How to mount a collage ready for framing

I like to sew my work onto mount board before I pass it onto a framer. This is how I do it:

Ingredients

- Acid-free mount/matt board in a pale colour
- Masking tape
- Thimble
- Needle and scissors

Method

- Cut the mount board to a size appropriate to the piece or frame. Allow at least 10cm (4in) all the way round and 12.5cm (5in) at the bottom.

- Double over a piece of masking tape and stick the back of your collage into position on the board. The border at the bottom should be bigger than the border at the top.

- Hold the collage down so it does not slip out of place and, wearing a thimble, poke holes with a sharp, strong, unthreaded needle through the collage and into the mount board. The holes should be at each corner and halfway along each side.

- Double up your thread and start to sew from the back, attaching the collage to the mount board with one tiny stitch using the holes as guides so that you do not inadvertently prick a piece of the border mount. Use a strong knot to start with and cover with masking tape so it does not come through to the top. Continue round the edge. It is likely you will run out of thread so make sure you cover the start and finish knot with tape. Half-way through try to remember to remove the folded up masking tape from underneath the collage, though it is not too much of a problem if you forget.

LEFT: Meta Heemskerk. *Rembrandt Collage*, 2012. 25 x 30cm (10 x 12in). This collage is mounted onto a piece of handmade paper which came from the oldest working paper mill in the Netherlands, dating back to the 17th century. It effectively links the mount to the historical nature of the Rembrandt collage.

MAKE

- Your piece is now ready to frame. Ask your framer to put a spacer or slip between the mount and glass, which means the textile will have space to breathe and will not be squished up against the glass. You could consider using old frames as **Claudia Rankin** does, but you might need to think ahead and make your collage to fit the frame rather than the other way round.

ABOVE: Claudia Rankin. *Little Black Cloud*, 2007. 30 x 24cm (12 x 8in). This hand-stitched collage was made in response to the flooding of a local river, which left all sorts of interesting bits in the high tide line, including bits of rubber and plastic, and a truly horrible, flowery nylon sleeping bag that Claudia used for the 'wings'. She effectively frames her work in recycled picture frames.

41

MAKE

Changing the scale

Going bigger

Textile collages can be made on any scale but bear in mind that if you plan to make something big like a wall hanging then you will need more fabric, more planning and more time to stitch it together and embellish.

When working on this scale I suggest either working onto a wall-sized piece of pin board or directly onto the floor. Work onto a base fabric (which might be pieced itself) and do not hurry. Indeed it is better to do it over several days and constantly re-evaluate the placing. Pin when you are happy with the composition and sew together in the same way as outlined in the previous section, attaching everything with holding stitches to the foundation fabric. This is not like quilt making where you might have templates, drawing and a plan. You are creating a unique visual language by working with layering and overlapping colours and textures. Your aim might be to create a harmonious blend but it could also be to create discordancy through your placement of colour or make the viewer's eye travel round the piece by repeating elements of colour or pattern or line.

Working on a larger scale brings with it the problem of where the focus of the piece is. The materials for textile collage can be hard to source and are of limited supply so you might wish to focus on creating a jewel-like feature within a large area of plain or textured fabric. In *Red Flowers at Night* the main background was made of old pieces of quilt that were overdyed black and then joined and layered. The quilts were so worn that quite a lot of wadding was exposed but because this was cotton it has dyed equally well and the textures created by the uneven wear and tear are integral to the piece. The bright area in the middle really pulls the eye in to the surface around the composition and was appliquéd on top of the base layer construction.

LEFT: *Red Flowers at Night* (detail). The red flowers are the focal point of this large wall hanging. They come from a worn piece of suzani embroidery from Uzbekistan.

ABOVE: *Red Flowers at Night*, 2013. 150 x 100cm (59 x 39in). This wall hanging is predominantly black but the eye is drawn in to the jewel-like section of bright collage which is echoed in the edging.

MAKE

Long – how to make a strippy fabric collage

At the end of a project you might have many tiny bits of fabric left which you feel are just too precious to throw away. These can be made into what I call a `strippy`. This is a nod towards strip patchwork techniques where strips of fabric are usually joined together by machine. In my version the strips and scraps are hand sewn onto a foundation and the edges are left raw rather than joined. Be selective, even though you are using the tiniest pieces of leftover fabric, and work within a colour scheme. The finished pieces can be mounted and framed or hung directly onto the wall or act as a starting point for another project.

OPPOSITE PAGE:
Strippy, 2015. 18 x 5cm (7 x 2in). The three stages of making a strippy collage – compose, pin, attach and embellish.

Ingredients

- Foundation fabric - a piece of bump, quilt or wool blanket.
- Tiny pieces of interesting fabric, lace, tapestry, buttons and trims
- Needle and thread
- Embroidery thread

Method

- Cut a small strip of foundation fabric, about 5 x 12cm (2 x 4¾in).

- The idea is initially to place strips of fabric across the foundation. These should be no more than 2cm (¾in) in height but do not all have to stretch the whole width of the fabric. Indeed your collage will be more interesting if you break up the arrangement with smaller shapes, rectangles and squares. Remember that this is collage not piecing so your components can slightly overlap or layer. Cut so that one vertical edge is straight but none of the foundation shows.

- Secure the collage with pins and sew together using either running stitches or tiny slip stitches so that everything is sewn onto the background.

- Embellish with a few embroidery stitches and perhaps a button or two.

MAKE

Small

Another use for those tiny leftover pieces is to turn them into mini collages for cards. You can work on several pieces at once, gathering scraps together into delightful little compositions, which can be glued onto blank greeting cards or postcards.

RIGHT AND BELOW: Tiny collages made from leftover scraps. Average size 6 x 4cm (2½ x 1½in).

MAKE

Appliqué

There is not really much difference between fabric collage and appliqué, which is defined as cutting pieces of one material and applying them to another. Creating a collaged background for appliqué can provide an interesting combination of rough edges and the more formal technique of finger turning. In *Red Flowers* a variety of fabrics including a piece of curtain fabric, a fraying bit of blanket and fabrics from an unpicked quilt have been attached using hand stitching to a piece of tweed. Onto this surface the flower and leaves have been appliquéd.

BELOW: *Red Flowers*, 2013. 18 x 20cm (7 x 8in). Finger-turned appliqué onto collaged backdrop.

MAKE

Finger-turned applique

This is the method often used in traditional quilts, particularly the spectacular nineteenth-century Baltimore quilts from the United States.

Ingredients

- Thin card and pencil
- Scissors
- Sewing threads
- **Cotton fabrics** – patchwork fabric and old, much washed shirts are ideal as is unpicked fabric from quilts if it is not too fragile.
- Pins, sewing threads and needles

Method

- Draw out your design to a scale that fits onto your foundation fabric. Use simple shapes that might be inspired by looking at folk art and embroidery designs or the way appliqué is used in traditional quilt making.

- Cut cardboard templates for each shape. I keep my appliqués really simple and basically use a lozenge shape, which can act as petals and leaves and also circles, half circles and hearts.

- Pin the card template to the fabric of your choice and cut the fabric out leaving a 1cm (⅓in) seam allowance.

- Notch any tight curves. This will help to ease the fabric into the round shape that you require.

- Remove the template and pin your piece of fabric to the background.

- Knot the sewing thread firmly and bring the thread up to the front. Starting on an 'easy' side of your shape, turn the fabric under 1cm (⅓in) and use a little slip stitch to hold the turn down. Make sure your thread matches the fabric colour. Continue to work round the shape, finger turning a little bit ahead and sewing down. You are drawing with your finger so be flexible. The shape might turn out a little bit different to how you planned! If you find it easier you could use running stitches but keep them really small so they are not intrusive.

- Work through, attaching all the appliqué pieces onto the background, making sure that you get them in the right order, so that if you have any layering you apply the piece underneath first.

MAKE

LEFT: *Strange Flowers*, 2015. 25 x 16cm (10 x 6in). Pieces of worn fabric are sewn onto a base of old quilt as a backdrop to these folk-inspired appliquéd flowers with chain-stitch stems.

There are many other methods of doing appliqué, which you can learn about in specialist books on the subject, but I feel this slow and traditional method suits the materials and style of my work. Of course, you do not have to do a fabric collage as a background to all appliqué. It can be done straight onto a piece of old quilt or another firm foundation fabric.

MAKE

Broderie perse

A variation of appliqué is the broderie perse (Persian embroidery) technique. A printed fabric with clearly defined areas is cut out and reapplied to a ground fabric to create a new design or scene. The finished appliquéd fabric would then be made into a coverlet or quilt. This technique originally used chintz fabric from India with its lovely flower and Oriental patterns but it could be done with anything with large-scale motifs. Broderie perse was usually done with turned edges but starch pastes were also used to stick it into place. You could, however, just cut out and apply with a little overstitch, blanket stitch, herringbone or a machine zigzag or use a transfer adhesive fabric such as Bondaweb to get your motifs firmly in place.

In *Stable Girl* an old curtain fabric was used. To stop the edges from fraying too much, Bondaweb was ironed onto the fabric before the motifs were cut out and attached with a slip stitch. The cut motifs were collaged together with bits of needlepoint and embellished with embroidery and buttons. The title for this piece was taken from the stories that surround the workaday tailors' sample quilts that provide the background for this wall piece. In the North East of England these were sometimes called 'stable boy quilts' because they might end up being used outside for the boy to sleep under, as a coverlet for a horse or bedding for the farm dog: a romantic myth perhaps.

LEFT: *Stable Girl*, 2012. 200 x 80cm (79 x 31½in). Broderie perse and applied needlepoint onto reclaimed patchwork quilt.

ABOVE: Detail of *Stable Girl* showing backstitch wool embellishment.

MAKE

Patchwork

You may have noticed that many of my own pieces incorporate small areas of patchwork. My addiction to stitching, and interest in patchwork and quilting, started in the late 1970s when I experimented with joining hexagons together over papers. At that time you could buy good-quality cotton offcuts from Laura Ashley and Liberty, which were perfect for the task. I have returned to this in my recent work, either sourcing old patchwork to use or making up sections myself to use within collages. These are not pieced into the composition but sit on the surface and are appliquéd onto the foundation using a slip stitch (sometimes called blind stitch) – you can see an example of this in *Spotted Star* on page 15.

You can buy templates for patchwork in specialist shops or download templates for hexagons, triangles and diamonds from the internet. Stick the downloaded paper onto card to make it more durable.

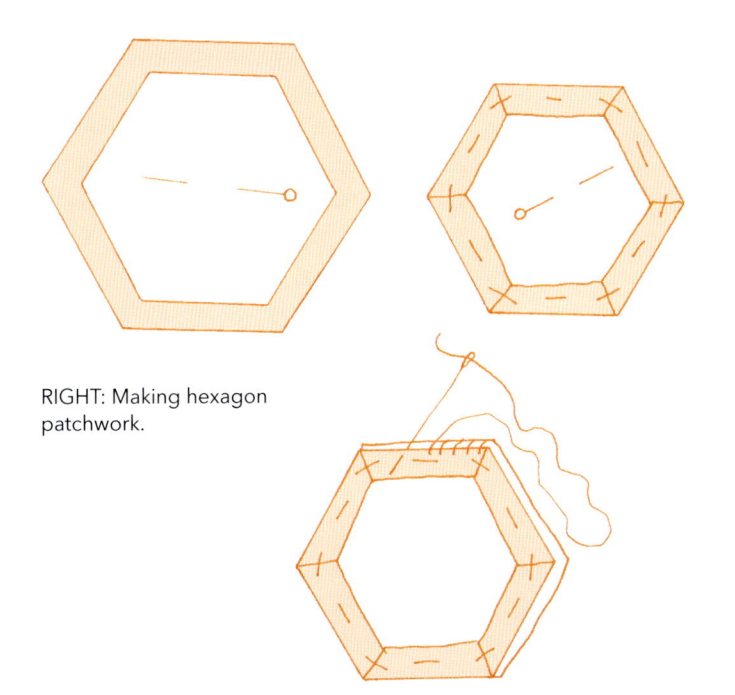

RIGHT: Making hexagon patchwork.

ABOVE: Finished hexagon flower with tacking still in place and diamonds tacked and ready to be sewn together to form a star.

Method

- Draw round the template onto thin paper.

- Pin the paper template onto the wrong side of a thin cotton-weight fabric and cut out, leaving a 1cm (⅓in) seam allowance.

- Thread up your needle with ordinary sewing thread with a strong knot at the end. Fold the right side of the fabric over the top of the template and pull the needle through both the paper and template. Work your way around the template folding in the corner flaps all in the same direction, as shown left. Finish with a secure knot.

- Join the separate elements together with an overstitch, as shown.

- Undo the tacking threads, carefully remove the papers and iron carefully. This is in order to keep the folded creases on the external edges of the patchwork in place.

- Appliqué onto your collage using a slip stitch, folding under flaps as you go.

MAKE

Mixing paper and cloth

Some artists pay homage to the original perception of collage as being a craft about paper and mix paper into their pieces or even use reinforced paper as the foundation for fabric collage.

Maria Thomas

Maria Thomas loves the tradition of scrap patchwork. She recognizes that it was a craft of necessity but she also sees underneath the practicalities to the meanings or memories that each scrap might have for the stitcher. She carries on the tradition through what she calls her 'quilts' but updates it to include items that have personal resonance to her but that most of us would discard. You might find beer bottle tops, sweet wrappers, price labels, pages from books and all manner of paper ephemera included in her pieces. They are deeply personal items that hold memories for Maria but may also resonate with those of us living contemporaneously.

Her use of paper within her collages refers directly back to the making of English patchwork where the backing papers are usually removed and discarded. Maria says that the paper is 'a huge part of the making process, the scaffolding of the quilt – the bit that the thought in the making is attached to, the heart of the work – and the fabric is the skin'.

She has developed her own way of mixing fabric and paper by bonding together two or three layers of paper and fabric with PVA. The fabric then becomes trapped in the middle or backed with paper and can be cut up as needed. Maria machine stitches the patchwork pieces then hand appliqués further elements, mixing with stitch and adding more found objects and decorations as she goes.

Spoon Fed Love is a response to the 'endearing' and enduring task of feeding her family. The spoons are a symbol of the constant giving that is required as a mother, not only through domesticity but metaphorically too. It houses very personal tokens relating to all three of her children, but at the same time there's a sense of it all happening before with the previous generations of mothers.

MAKE

BELOW: Maria Thomas. *Spoon Fed Love* (detail), 2011. 40 x 180cm (16 x 71in). Found fabric and paper, machine patchwork with hand appliqué and quilting.

MAKE

Cas Holmes

Cas Holmes trained in fine art and works between the disciplines of painting, drawing and textiles. Salvaged materials are torn, cut and reassembled to create mixed-media pieces, which draw their inspiration from 'hidden' or 'overlooked' observations of daily life. *Unfolding Landscape: Spring Verge* is one of a series looking at the changing seasons of roadside/railway/footpath verges and a reflection of the flora and fauna dependent on these small areas in our urban spaces. The materials have been collected as she travels and the piece reflects the 'rawness' of these discarded remnants. Cas writes: 'The places where our gardens meet the greater landscape and the relationship between "Urban" and "Nature" has been informed by stories of my Romany grandmother, old and forgotten textiles, and the natural cycle of growth, decay and renewal. Working with "stitch sketching", I seek to capture a moment or thing before it is gone.'

In this piece paper has been printed and painted with plant forms and then bonded to fragmented cloth layers with a dilute cellulose paste. This is intended as a temporary hold allowing her to add additional detail with free-motion and hand stitch. As she works the fabric softens. Further drawing and mark making with paint often happens at this stage and then the piece is 'auditioned' or hung to enable final stitching and seams go into place. This determines the drape and fold.

ABOVE: Cas Holmes. *Unfolding Landscape: Spring Verge*, 2015. 200 x 90cm (80 x 35in). Mixed media.

MAKE

This chapter has encouraged you to work in an intuitive way with colour and composition, using a wide variety of fabrics with surface interest and texture, or that are old and have a story to tell of their own. The techniques described can be applied to other projects. Examples have been given of the way I and other artists make and use the fabric collage, and you now need to develop your own way of working in response to your own collection of materials.

55

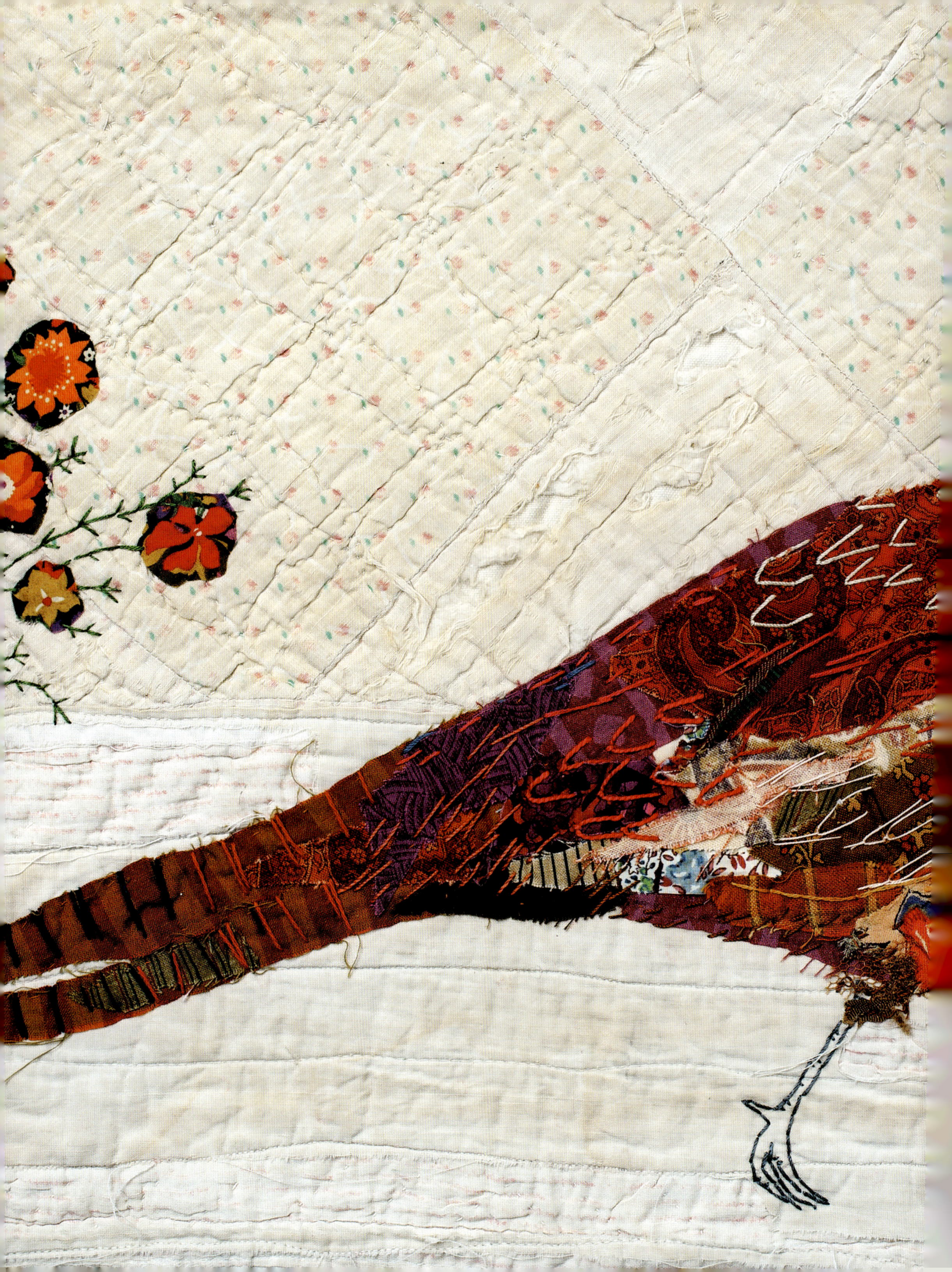

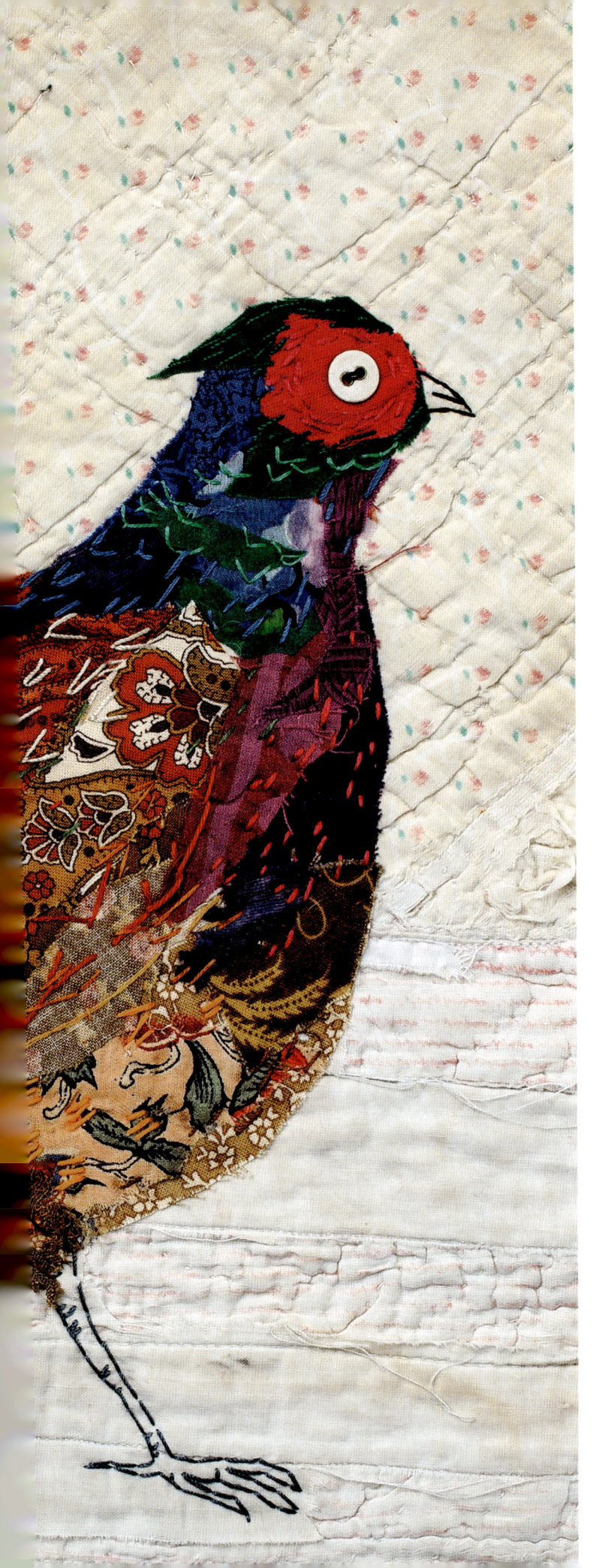

PORTRAY

So far the fabric collage technique has been described in relation to creating abstract compositions, but it can also be used to create portraits of people, animals and birds. The collage approach allows the freedom to use fabrics almost to paint a picture with fabric and thread. This can be challenging but you might be rewarded with a representation that is unusual, charming and captures character in the way that paint or traditional art media might not be able to do.

LEFT: *Pheasant*, 2015. 32 x 45cm (12 x 18in). Tiny scraps of fabric are used to build up the rich plumage of this pheasant with stitching giving added surface interest.

PORTRAY

Enchanted forest

I started developing my 'Enchanted Forest' series of work after encountering an adult stag, standing very still, on a path in a country park built over a disused coal mine in the middle of a conurbation. I was excited to see something so wild and intensely beautiful so close and in the city, and it reminded me of those small thrills that you get every time you see a hare running across a field, a squirrel hastily retreating into the foliage of a tree or deer gathering at dusk. I was indeed enchanted and went home to look at pictures in books, did a few sketches, and then was off on my own journey into the forest trying to create portraits of other undomesticated animals and birds.

Artists have always taken inspiration from the natural world. In most cultures small creatures and wild beasts can be found depicted in a range of styles from folk art to fine art, in interior decoration and architecture, and on ceramics and textiles. Stone Age people depicted their prey on the walls of their caves and in medieval times mythical beasts such as unicorns graced tapestries. We still use the wallpaper and furnishing fabrics that William Morris designed in the nineteenth century, and which are full of birds, plants and animals. In the twenty-first century a new generation of printmakers and artists such as Mark Hearld, Angela Harding and Rob Ryan have led the resurgence in nature imagery appearing on everything from mugs, bedcovers and curtains to stationery. Animals and birds are still at the centre of many children's stories and picture books and many of us grew up with Beatrix Potter and *The Wind in the Willows*, and were captivated by the white rabbit always appearing at the edges of *Alice's Adventures in Wonderland*. Even if we did not grow up in the countryside and have not had the chance to make acquaintance with wild creatures, we are still aware of them and learn to identify them through books, cartoons and even through seeing stuffed exhibits in natural history museums.

The important thing is not to copy but to learn from this connection and to develop your own visual language and style to make work that is original and based on techniques that you love. I have tried to do this by mixing pieces of quilt with textile collage techniques to produce a series of wild animal portraits.

RIGHT: *Deer*, 2013. 24 x 24cm (9½ x 9½in). Small areas of fabric collage highlight the contours in this portrait and the stitching provides a strong silhouette.

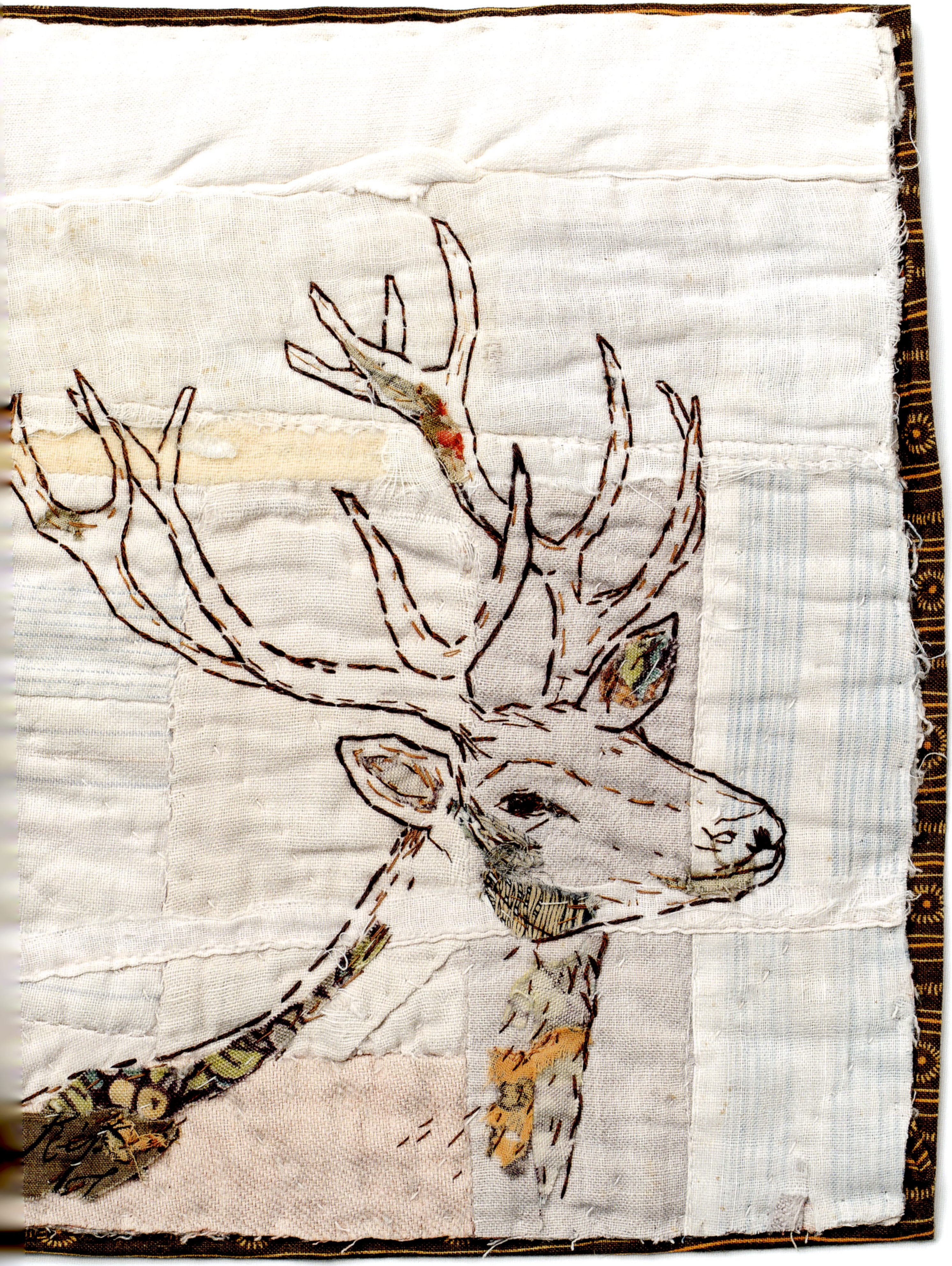

PORTRAY

Making templates and drawings

BELOW: Transfer monotype drawing.

OPPOSITE: *Grey Wolf*, 2013. 30 x 21cm (12 x 8in). Long and short stitches, over the collaged areas, follow the direction of the fur growth.

Very few of us are able to get close to wild animals to get a photographic record or to do an observational drawing so we have to rely on memory, or an image found in a book, to give us the information we need to build up a portrait. If you can do a drawing, even from a photo, this will enable you to capture the key elements in a personal way rather than relying on someone else's interpretation. What is important is good colour reference and a template showing a strong silhouette.

Silhouette is the most important part of getting it right. You can use as many fabrics as you like to build up colour but if the basic shape and form is not recognizable then it will not work. I have collected images for a long time from a variety of sources such as magazines, the internet, leaflets and printmaking and store these in plastic sleeves dedicated to each species. I particularly love scientific illustration from the past and the work of engravers such as George-Louis Leclerc, Comte de Buffon and Thomas Bewick and natural history painters such as John James Audubon. These help me in terms of colour and line and I will sometimes produce my own drawings from these source materials to help me get to know the form of the head and to capture expressions and the character of the beast. I often work with the transfer monotype process. I ink up a Perspex plate with a roller and printmaking ink, ensuring I have a very thin layer of evenly rolled out ink. I attach an image from a magazine or a photograph from the internet to a sheet of paper with tape and then tape the paper over the plate with the image facing upwards. I draw with a biro or pencil through the image, choosing which lines I want to emphasise. When I pull the paper away from the plate the ink has transferred onto the paper where I have made the marks and made what I consider an original drawing, as I have decided what marks to make. These simple drawings are really useful in giving me the information about the way the fur lies, the markings on the animal and where the eyes and nose are placed.

I have made up a library of templates, which I share with students and use again and again. For example I might blow up a Victorian engraving on a photocopier and then stick it onto firm card and I have a shape to draw round. This is a bit like the process of making appliqué templates. The template is drawn round with a water-soluble pen onto fabric and when the collage is complete the marking is removed with water and a clean paintbrush.

PORTRAY

PORTRAY

Building up your collage

RIGHT: The cardboard template was drawn around with a water-soluble pen then tiny bits of fabric are layered within the outline and pinned in place before being attached.

Ingredients

- Foundation fabric – a piece of old quilt is ideal but it might be a piece of tweed or a fabric tacked onto wadding or bonded curtain lining (bump).
- Water-soluble pen
- Cardboard template of animal or bird
- Fabrics
- Pins and needles
- Sewing and embroidery threads

Method

- Draw round the template with the water-soluble pen. Freely draw extra detailing such as eyes, chin outline, haunches. Refer to your drawing, computer or book image.

- Assemble a palette of small pieces of fabric within the colour scheme of your subject. Do not feel these have to be plain fabrics but use patterns, lace, sheers and a variety of types and weights of fabric.

- Start to cut pieces to build up tone and colour to as near the shape of the silhouette as you can. I usually start with the back of the animal, which is the strongest line. Cut roughly or tear so that you do not have any ugly straight edges. You may have to use very small pieces to fit into intricate shapes. Be aware that the underbelly of an animal is often of a lighter colour than the back and reflect this in your choice of scraps.

- Start by just laying on the top fabrics and roughly overlapping but pin down if you feel your components are starting to move. You do not have to cover the whole of the background but could leave some areas of the base fabric showing through as I did.

- When you have all your fabrics pinned then you need to sew them on. Use a small 'holding' or stab stitch in matching thread. Make it as small and invisible as possible. These are not tacking stitches and will not be taken out later. They can be up to 1.5cm (½in) apart so long as they effectively keep everything in place. Change the colour of the thread if necessary.

Stitching

Your stitches should echo the way you would stroke an animal or bird. Unless you really wanted to upset it, you would stroke from head through to rump and your embroidery should follow this general direction. You will use mostly long and short stitch, couching, seeding and perhaps detached chain and feather stitch if you are doing a bird. I use a pure silk, stranded and perle threads. Change the colours of your threads and use them to create contour and to blend over the edges of the fabric. Use backstitch and satin stitch to define the eye rather than collaging on a lifeless, flat piece of fabric. If the eye area is big enough you might want to attach a tiny coloured piece of fabric for the iris. If your beast looks as though it is merging too much into the background then you might need to use backstitch to outline it.

RIGHT: Detail of *Grey Wolf* showing long and short stitches in a variety of threads. These follow the contours of the fur and are used to blend the edges of the fabric.

PORTRAY

Finishing

ABOVE: *Fox and Flowers*, 2015. 27 x 21cm (10½ x 8in). Tiny flowers have been cut out and attached to the background with a little overstitch.

I sometimes finish my pieces by adding some foliage or flowers to contextualize the animal. I cut these out, leaving raw edges and sew on with an overstitch. Edges of the foundation fabric are usually left raw to echo the collaging of the fabrics within the central image.

RIGHT: *Spring Hare*, 2015. 24 x 18cm (9½ x 7in). A template was drawn round to give a silhouette which has been stitched using mostly backstitch and long and short stitch.

Line

An alternative approach to using tiny scraps of fabric to build up a full-bodied portrait is to concentrate on line qualities. It is important that you have a strong picture reference to work from when using this technique, ideally a line drawing such as those produced by Victorian engravers or a very detailed photograph. Choose a foundation that will not distract too much from the line drawing that you are going to make over the top. Make a template, as above, to draw around to give you the basic outline, but instead of using fabric this time you are going to use pure stitch to describe the animal. I use three strands of embroidery floss to work up the main silhouette and go down to two or even one strand for the finer details. Work up the design mostly in backstitch but look closely at your picture reference and try to make your stitches similar to the marks made by the artist. Do not necessarily use one long line of backstitch but leave little gaps, almost like skipped stitches or work the stitches slanting.

You can create an environment for the animal or bird through collaging fabrics into the background and applying stitches to suggest branches or stems.

ABOVE: *Deer*, 2015. 18 x 18cm (7 x 7in). This delicate deer has been sewn onto a section of an old log cabin quilt. As for the *Spring Hare*, above, a context for the animal has been created with the appliquéd flowers and chain stitch stems.

PORTRAY

ABOVE: Karen Nicol. *Deer Girl*, 2014. 80 x 90cm (31½ x 35½in). Karen uses an Irish Singer embroidery machine to couch vintage treasures onto the deer.

PORTRAY

Animal magic

Karen Nicol

Karen Nicol is a London-based fashion embroiderer and designer who has worked for forty years creating couture embroidery detailing for well-known fashion designers and has latterly developed her personal practice. She works in her home studio in London, which is a mood board itself, full of objects she has collected for years from flea markets and car boot sales and which provide an enriching backdrop to her ideas. She has built up a vast collection of beads, lace, haberdashery, fabric and jewellery, which is integrated into the animal and bird portraits that she creates, and her unusual approach is admired in both the fine art and textile worlds.

Nicol is constantly experimenting to find new ways to create textured surfaces, which involve working directly with manipulated materials, but also refer to historic textile techniques. Her vocabulary and knowledge of stitches in combination with this constant investigative approach to surface decoration produces amazing results when applied to representing animals and birds. She does not, however, stray far from the source of inspiration in her careful choice of materials. *White Stag* was created for a solo show in New York called 'The Edge of the Woods' in 2014. Based on grosgrain and silk velvet the stag and birds are embroidered using free-motion machine embroidery and hand stitching. The stag has a hand-painted glass eye, horse hair in the ear and fabric-covered 'leaf' background. For *Deer Girl* Nicol adapted the traditional technique of couching for her Irish Singer embroidery machine around vintage treasures for the deer markings. The bird is embroidered with free-motion machine embroidery, as is the face and neck of the deer with a hand-painted glass eye. Bonded chiffon creates the dappled leaf ground.

ABOVE: Karen Nicol. *White Stag*, 2014. 100 x 100cm (39 x 39in). Embroidered and painted silk.

Birds

Birds have always been there at the edge of my vision and as a child on my plate. I spent most of my childhood messing about on a farm in Norfolk and one of my earliest memories was throwing grain to chickens and collecting eggs. Pheasants were, and still are to me, exotic creatures who strutted across empty fields but, along with wild ducks, they arrived at the back door upside down and limp, having been shot by my grandad. My grandmother would hang them up in the dairy and then after a week or two they would be plucked in the barn and make an appearance for Sunday dinner. Now I am out of touch with this country lifestyle and have to be satisfied with observing the behaviour of the everyday birds that surround me in the city. There is always a pigeon cooing somewhere on a rooftop nearby, a seagull squawking above and, on my allotment, the sweeter sounds of the robin, wren and blackbird. I am drawn to these common birds, which can be encountered every day, and other artists have been too as they have been celebrated and depicted in art for hundreds of years or more.

PORTRAY

One of my favourite books is *Thomas Bewick's Book of Birds* (1797). I can just about see the rooftop of his birthplace, Cherryburn, from my studio window, which overlooks the Tyne Valley in Northumberland. The book may be more than 200 years old, but Bewick's wood engravings of land and water birds arose from personal observation of the creatures that surrounded him: he had an intimate knowledge, which was unsurpassed, and the book is still an important point of reference. It delights me to know that the great American bird painter John James Audubon came over to Great Britain to meet Bewick, as Audubon's studies of birds and animals are also a great inspiration to me.

The Wren is my attempt to work up in stitch a homage to Bewick's study of the wren. I transferred the image using typewriter carbon paper. I taped the carbon, ink side down, onto my painted fabric, and then taped a photocopy of the wood engraving over that. I did not make a detailed tracing but just tried to put in the main lines to give me an accurate silhouette on the fabric. Using one or two strands of thread I attempted to re-create Bewick's marks with the wood-cut tools. Bewick's birds were always shown sitting in a landscape or habitat and I could not attempt to reproduce that but I have used a few wisps of fabric and embroidery to create some sort of background.

Sometimes the birds I produce are less realistic and the design is drawn from observing many stylized birds – in ethnic textiles such as Indian and African appliquéd textiles and on old appliquéd quilts from the United States. In homage to the great tradition of appliqué I make templates of the different parts of the bird – the body, the tail, the wing, the head – and then pin the templates onto cotton fabric scraps. I cut the fabric out leaving a 1cm (⅓in) seam allowance all the way round. The pieces are sewn onto the fabric using the traditional finger-turned technique and then embellished with stitch.

OPPOSITE: *The Wren (after Thomas Bewick)*, 2015. 30 x 22cm (12 x 9in). Image transferred, using typewriter carbon paper, onto a painted and tea-dyed background. A tiny amount of collage, including a section of a handkerchief, has been applied and delicate fern stitches suggest twigs.

ABOVE: These birds have been appliquéd onto old pieces of quilt using the finger-turned appliqué technique described on page 48.

69

PORTRAY

Louise Saxton

Louise Saxton, an Australian artist, works on a large scale using reclaimed domestic detritus and textiles, transforming the tiniest elements into dramatic assemblages. The pieces, which have been exhibited in prestigious Australian galleries, refer to the preoccupation of the fine artists and illustrators of the past with depicting flora and fauna. She effectively mixes art and craft through reinventing and bringing to life details from what is considered fine art but using fragments of textiles that have been defined as craft. Everyday needlework created in domestic settings by previous generations will become as rare as some of the species depicted, as the craft techniques are forgotten and as the pieces themselves become harder to find. The fabric fragments are often well worn through use and Louise has developed a technique whereby the pieces are combined subtly using lace pins. She writes: 'The use of pins rather than stitching or gluing emphasises the fragility of the materials, the domestic needlework traditions and species in the natural world. The pins also add to the sculptural nature of the works, which are either set in relief or three-dimensional.'

Major Tom is part of a series of work called 'Sanctuary' and is based on her study of a painting by John and Elizabeth Gould (*c*.1848). Louise makes the link between the hiddenness of needlework in the home and the storage of artworks in museums. Many natural history paintings, prints and drawings are hidden away too, rarely seen by the public, and she draws attention to this archival material, which depicts birds and insects that are too becoming extinct.

LEFT: Louise Saxton. *Major Tom* (detail above), 2010. After J & E Gould *c*.1848. 103 x 49cm (41 x 19in). Reclaimed needlework, lace pins, nylon tulle.

RIGHT: *Harvest*, 2014. 29 x 28cm (11½ x 11in). Tiny scraps of fabric are patched onto a faded checked fabric which has been attached, log cabin style, around the central image. Wheatear stitch and lazy daisy-stitched flowers have been worked onto the surface.

People portraits

A portrait is a likeness of a person. I do not use the word 'likeness' casually as the best portraits capture the personality and the mood of the person while sometimes they may not be accurate representations. They make us want to know more about the person and, at one time, before photography was invented, paintings were the only record of how people looked.

I do not have enough experience in figurative drawing to try to do portraits myself, even using cloth and stitch, but I do have a curiosity about people and the lives they led or might have led. For years I have collected old photographs, which I have picked up cheaply from flea markets and vintage bookshops. I look through these regularly and try to get some clues about the person from how they are dressed, the background context and sometimes, if I am lucky, I am rewarded with a name and date on the back of the photograph. There is a little bit of mystery about these images as we do not really know who they are and we can impress our own ideas of their characters and back stories onto the photographs. These found photographs and old postcards can be used as a focal point in a collage. You can tell a little story through the fabrics you choose and capture the viewer's imagination in the same way as when the image initially engaged you.

Transferring the image onto cloth

I have approached the construction of these portrait collages in different ways but in all instances I transfer the image onto fabric first. There are many ways of doing this but I always use the method that uses purchased iron-on transfer paper. This comes in packs of several sheets and there is one sort for light fabrics and another for dark. This specialist paper is now easily available through the internet or from large stationers and computer-paper suppliers. The paper is treated on one side with a heat-sensitive silicone film and the image is transferred by ironing or using a heat press. You put the paper in your computer printer tray and print your image onto the paper. It is really important to print your image in reverse by either pressing the mirror image or reverse icon within the printer settings or rotating horizontally through Photoshop before you go to print. When the image is printed on the transfer paper follow the manufacturer's instructions carefully. Most manufacturers recommend turning off the steam on your iron, ironing onto a flat hard surface rather than a cushioned ironing board and keeping the iron moving. The instructions will tell you which heat setting to use, how long to iron for and how to pull the transfer paper off the fabric. This will vary depending on the exact product.

Portrait collage build-up

I am very much led in the collage build-up by the colour of the photograph. This gives me direction to which fabrics and colour scheme I should use and sometimes also the style of the piece. The response to a Victorian sepia photograph might be to use faded, washed-out colours with maybe a bit of lace. A 1950s style image would tempt me to use a much brighter palette.

In *Harvest* on page 71, the tinted photograph and the clothes of the girl suggested autumnal colours with a slightly workwear look to the fabrics. The image was tacked onto a calico support fabric and then the pink check surrounding fabric with the frayed edge was sewn round the image with a stab stitch. An old French striped fabric was placed behind the calico and pulled round to the front and to create a frame, with the edges turned under and sewn down. The formality of the edges was softened with little patchwork pieces informally sewn across the border of the central and framing fabrics. The subject matter of the portrait has suggested the stitching, with wheatear stitch and lazy daisy flowers in different thicknesses spilling out of the photo.

A quicker method of attaching fabrics would be to use Bondaweb (transfer adhesive). I do not use this regularly because it can add a stiffness to the work, which I do not favour. If I want to add machine embroidery, however, then the stiff bonded surface can be an advantage as you do not need to use an embroidery hoop. *Remember Me* was built up using this technique. This process is explained overleaf.

OPPOSITE: *Remember Me* (teaching sample), 2014. 42 x 28cm (16½ x 11in). The fabrics in this collage were attached to the calico base using Bondaweb. Unusually, for me, there are elements of machine embroidery and other embellishment.

Remember Me

PORTRAY

Making a collage with Bondaweb

Ingredients

- A3 piece of foundation fabric, e.g. cotton sheeting or calico
- A3 piece of Bondaweb
- Selection of collage fabrics
- Image already transferred onto a separate piece of fabric
- Scissors
- Iron
- Baking parchment

Method

- Place your foundation fabric onto your ironing board and set your iron to a hot setting.

- Iron the Bondaweb onto the fabric so the fabric and Bondaweb are stuck together. Make sure you are ironing the paper side with the glue facing the fabric or the Bondaweb will stick to the iron.

- Allow to cool, then peel back the paper layer to expose the thin layer of dry glue sitting on the surface of the fabric.

- Choose a position for your photograph and lay it onto the foundation fabric.

- Using small bits of fabric start to build up the collage onto the foundation fabric. Do not worry about overlapping areas that are not exposed to the glue on the foundation fabric. Just cut small bits of Bondaweb, pull away the paper and push the remaining fragile layer of glue under the layered fabrics so they will stick when ironed. Do not use heavyweight fabrics when building up a collage using this method. It is unlikely the Bondaweb, which is designed for bonding lightweight cottons together, will be effective in sticking the heavier fabric in place.

- When you have achieved a pleasing arrangement turn the iron back on. To avoid glue being transferred onto your iron, and to protect the coating on the transferred image, place a piece of silicone paper or baking parchment (found in supermarkets) over the top of your work and iron through this.

- Allow to cool, remove the protective paper and you will find that all of your collage pieces have been lightly attached to the backing fabric.

You may still have to use some additional holding stitches if some pieces have not properly adhered. You can continue to layer up, with heavier fabrics and maybe trims and lace, but this is certainly a speedy way of attaching collage pieces so that you have more time to spend on the stitching. In *Remember Me* both hand and machine embroidery were used to enhance the surface of the piece and add texture.

ABOVE: Lazy daisy flowers on backstitch stems stretch across *Remember Me* (see page 73). Choose thread colours that complement your fabric selection.

PORTRAY

Collaged portraits

OPPOSITE: Sue Stone. 63 • A Self Portrait • No. 14. 25.5 x 30.5cm (10 x 12in). Appliqué, hand and machine stitching.

Some textile artists excel in creating self-portraits or portraits of friends and family, or even historical figures, using only fabric and thread. The fabrics used to describe hair, clothes and skin tone are carefully selected and stitch used with sensitivity to describe the form of the figure.

Sue Stone

Sue Stone started her portrait series after she was asked to produce something other than a straightforward self-portrait for an exhibition in her home town of Grimsby. It has led to a massive commitment to do 63 self-portraits, one for each year of her life. She uses photographs as *aides-mémoire* to start her off but she does not slavishly copy them. Indeed there are periods in her life where she has no photographs of her life, only self-portrait drawings to go from.

The backgrounds are natural linen. Sometimes Sue does a simple drawing onto this to establish where the centre of the eyes, the nose and top lip are placed on the canvas. She starts with the eyes but she is always trying to capture the character and feeling of the time of the photograph and is not aiming for likeness. The hand stitching of the contours and form of the face is not over worked but spare and thoughtful with an almost illustrative quality. The clothing is a mixture of new and recycled fabrics and these collage elements are again sewn on both by hand and machine. If at all possible she will try to incorporate pieces of her own clothing that she has kept. She sometimes creates interesting textures through her use of strip or needle weaving.

Sue is attempting to describe through the textile collages the feelings she was experiencing at the time of the self-portrait and the whole series will capture both the ups and downs of her life. All have strap lines stitched to the side of the stretched canvas, which relate to personal events and memories. The process so far has been cathartic. Sue has learnt to be resilient against the feelings that arise through revisiting years that were difficult. This is a brave project, which has called for self-examination and re-living of painful, as well as happy, times but it has an integrity we can all learn from in producing our own version of the self-portrait.

ABOVE: Sue Stone. 63 • A Self Portrait • No. 4. 25.5 x 30.5cm (10 x 12in). Appliqué, hand and machine stitching.

PORTRAY

Emily Jo Gibbs originally had a successful career as an accessories designer but since 2009 has been working on sensitive hand-embroidered portraits of her family and friends. Her work is very personal and many of her pieces contain text with messages to her children, or reflect on parenting or relationships. She works up the collages from photographs and uses multiple layers of silk organza, which are hand stitched using mercerized cotton. They are tacked together before she starts to use hand stitches to create lines and marks. She likes the flat, matt qualities of the organza and the ordinary sewing thread. About Slaley she writes: 'At the bottom of Sasha's garden beyond the long grass and the stream, there is a shed on stilts. The perfect place for hiding out and playing pirates.'

Louise Baldwin and **Rosie James** both use sewing machines in the construction of their work. Their work relies on line and silhouette to describe the character. Rosie's figures are drawn from photographs of people walking around Chatham. The figures are drawn onto tissue paper first and then stitched onto cloth. The tissue paper is then removed. The striped fabric, cut-out figures are Bondawebbed onto the background. The threads from the stitched figures are left loose and pulled straight to extend the line from the stitched figure to link in with the striped figure. The work shown here is a sample exploring the lines of connection between us when in a city or crowd, the lines of the city streets, the telegraph lines above us, and lines of maps mapping our routes through the streets.

ABOVE: Emily Jo Gibbs. *Slaley*, 2014. 63 x 53cm (25 x 21in). Linen, silk organza applique, hand stitch.

PORTRAY

ABOVE: Rosie James. *Stripe Sample*, 2015. 19 x 28cm (8 x 11in). Recycled men's shirting with stitch drawing in blue thread.

ABOVE: Louise Baldwin. *Glance*, 2014. 43 x 45cm (17 x 18in). Fabrics attached with an embellisher, hand and machine stitch.

Louise Baldwin chooses not to uses Bondaweb as she finds it hard to sew through. She creates her backgrounds by using an embellisher, which mashes the fabrics together and holds them down. Her faces are a combination of drawing and working from photos. They are usually of no one in particular but often have a line down the bottom lip: Louise's daughter managed to split her lip when she was little and has a tiny scar across her bottom lip, which Louise finds intriguing and like a piece of hidden history in the face.

This chapter has encouraged you to use textile collage techniques to create more figurative work. You will need to draw or research images to work from and use your fabrics and stitch to build up a recognisable portrait. You may wish to pursue a more linear approach or use your collections of fabrics to build up a portrait that uses cloth to describe the colour or texture of an animal, bird or person.

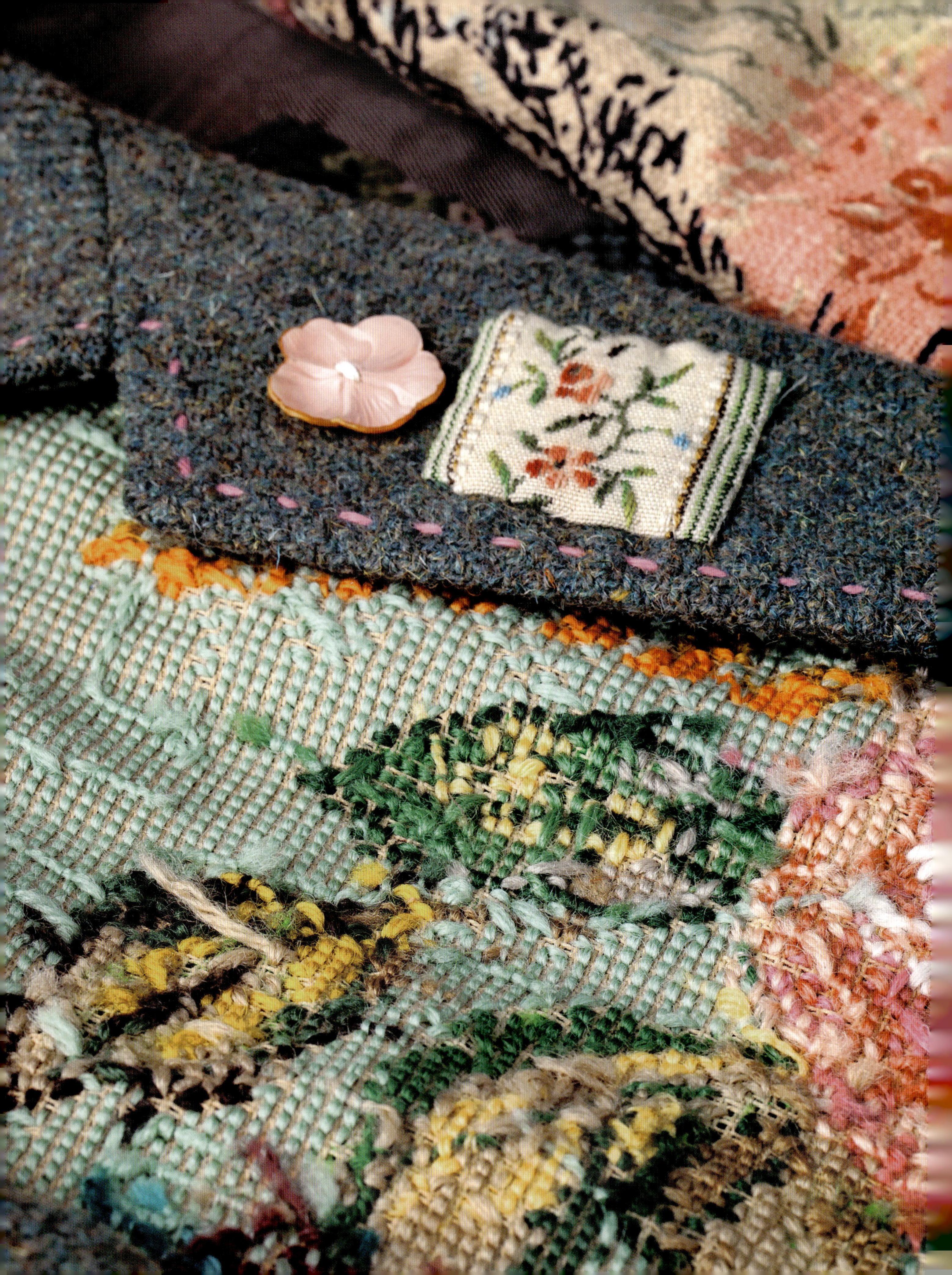

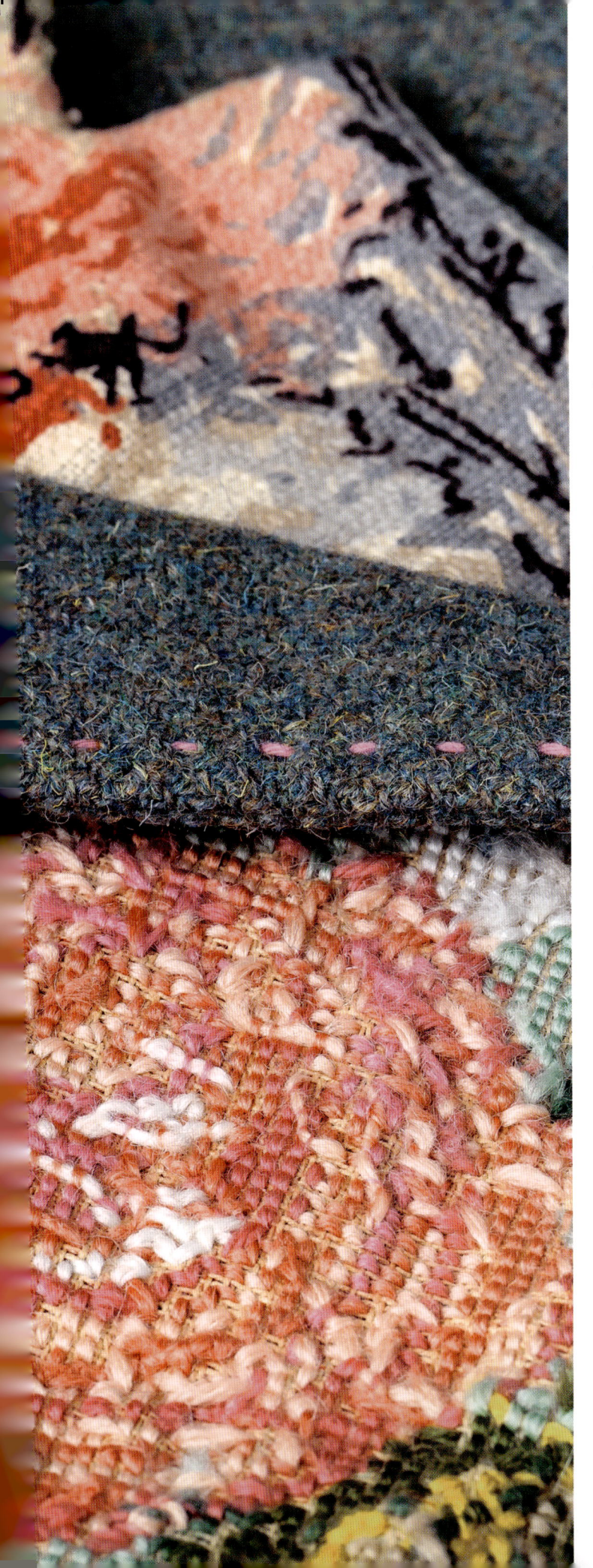

WORN

Rescued garments and accessories make great blank canvases onto which to assemble a collage of different types of fabrics, trimmings and stitches. They can be customized and embellished to be used as wearable art or can be hung on the wall as a backdrop to your lifestyle, just as you would hang a painting. Clothes have always been used as signifiers of taste and you can work into a pre-loved garment without dressmaking skills, conveying your personal aesthetic and individuality. You can transform an item, by incorporating references through the scraps and the fabrics you choose, to capture memories of other times and places and people. In our throwaway culture and where there are mounting concerns over the production of cheap clothes, garment collage is a great eco and upcycling technique.

LEFT: Detail of collar and applied needlepoint on upcycled tweed jacket.

What to use

You need to pick something you love in terms of colour, fabric or cut or which has personal resonance for you. I find it difficult to work with synthetic fabrics and look for classic clothes that might be slightly out of fashion but are made from quality wool, cotton or silk. It is more interesting to use something old, which has a bit of history and has had a past life. The most special garments might come from someone who has passed on, or might be from your own past, even your childhood. Bear in mind that even if something is really past its use-by date, such as old shirts that are worn round the collar, you can still use the fabrics within them for patchwork projects or bringing onto the surface of something else. Always try to use a clean garment. If it is something you cannot machine wash then you may have to get it dry cleaned first.

Look out for the following items in thrift shops, car boot sales and markets:

- **Jackets.** Great to use to embellish (see page 86), but also to deconstruct, which exposes the inner workings of the tailor.

- **Children's and dolls' clothes.** These are immediately evocative of times past as we, as adults, look back to our youth. The small size may mean you have a smaller canvas to work on and can present different challenges as you will need to select the embellishment more carefully, given the smaller area on which to place it.

- **Skirts and petticoats.** You can utilize both the hems and the waistbands.

- **Gloves.** Difficult to sew through but lots of potential in the cuff area.

- **Blouses and shirts.** Look for items from both men and women. Cuffs, lapels and the button-through parts offer scope for little patchworked areas and stitch details.

- **Dresses.** Wedding dresses, evening dresses, very worn everyday dresses. A hand-me-down or dress you have kept from a significant part of your life can be an expressive device through which you explore memories, either pleasurable or painful.

- **Underwear and corsets.** You can have fun with these. Look at the work of Julia Triston whose series of quirky Bra-Ra dresses took her to the fourth plinth of Trafalgar Square!

- **Collars.** I have sometimes utilized these by embroidering words onto the inside of collars, which are hidden once worn.

- **Knitwear.** Difficult to attach fabric to but great to embroider onto with wool or appliqué with felt.

If you are going to wear the garment it is important to find something that fits you but if you are making something to hang up or frame then the aesthetic of the piece is of more concern than size.

LEFT: Children's garments ready for embellishment.

WORN

Getting started

Once you have selected a garment to work with the next stage is to gather together all the materials you think you will use in the project. The colour, texture and possibly the use of print on the garment will affect your choices, and you should choose fabrics, trims and embroidery threads that complement and blend with the garment. There is usually one key piece of fabric from which you can work up your colour palette, e.g. a special piece of needlepoint or found embroidery that you definitely want to use as embellishment. Make a pile of these potential components, which could include furnishing and fashion fabrics, buttons, trims, lace, found embroidery and tweed. You might also use pieces from other garments, e.g. pockets, cuffs and manufacturers' labels. They might not get used, but having them together to choose from is an essential part of the selection and design process.

Lay the pieces over the garment, cutting down to appropriate sizes then pin on to see how the colours and textures interplay with each other and how the application affects the 'hang' of the garment. Do not let the decoration overwhelm. Leave some areas free of embellishment to allow the original garment to show through and have its own voice. It is useful to hang the garment up so you can see it from a distance. Leave overnight and keep reviewing.

You can attach the collage ingredients with slip stitch or you can turn the edges and hem. Turning the edges is a good idea if you intend to wear the garment as it will prevent fraying. Once you have attached the fabric bits, consider the embroidery. Unlike the textile collages described earlier in the book you may not need to blend the fabrics with stitch but instead use stitch to decorate and make a statement. You might have an area of dense stitching or you might follow the line of a hem, cuff or lapel.

RIGHT: A work in progress – tiny pieces of fabric have been inserted into the backstitch leaf shapes, while the striped fabric and trim might be used on the collar and yoke.

WORN

WORN

RIGHT: *Kilt Jacket.* Tweed jacket embellished with needlepoint, a dressing-gown pocket detail, patchwork and buttons.

Jackets

Traditional tweed jackets are a joy to work with, but can be expensive especially if they have the 'Harris Tweed' label inside. Uniform jackets, kilt jackets and women's tweed jackets can also be used. You can decorate the lapels, the pockets, the elbows and sleeves, the cuffs, the front, the back and the inside. Pockets on jackets have lots of potential and can provide a focal point to pull the viewer in.

An example is given here of the build-up of collage and stitch onto two jackets. The key piece I wanted to use on the Scottish kilt jacket, because it shared the same soft colours of the tweed, was a bit of old needlepoint I had taken out of a frame. It has been applied with the back of the stitching exposed as this had more surface interest. The colours of the other fabrics, which include French toile, a bit of unpicked quilt and tweed, were

WORN

LEFT: *The Mona Lisa Jacket* embellished with applied curtain fabric (broderie perse technique) and needlepoint.

carefully selected to carry on the colour story and mood. When I was sure that everything worked together, I cut the appliqué pieces more accurately and in this case added a seam allowance so that I could turn the edges of some of the fabrics. Everything was stitched on by hand using a tiny overstitch and a double thread for strength as I anticipated the jacket actually being worn.

The next stage was the stitching. A soft cotton sashiko thread was used for most of the stitching, which has been kept very simple, just running and cross stitches. Lastly I have changed the buttons. I do this with most of the garments I use as it gives me the chance to delve into my button box and perhaps use vintage buttons that cannot be commonly found. You could make your own covered buttons as I have done for *The Mona Lisa Jacket*.

The Mona Lisa Jacket uses the broderie perse technique. Flower motifs from an old pair of curtains have been appliquéd onto the front. The floral theme has been continued with the application of a piece of needlepoint, which has been used on the lapels and the pockets. Pieces of unpicked quilt and other tweed scraps have also been used. All were sewn on with discreet overstitches. A hidden feature is a Mona Lisa needlepoint, which is on the inside back of the jacket and only revealed when the jacket is unbuttoned. There is a small amount of decorative stitching using tapestry wool and large running stitches.

Jan Knibbs

Jan Knibbs is a fashion and textile designer who creates amazing items of wearable art, all adorned with her distinctive signature style of rich, hand-worked embroidery. She collages vintage fabrics, offcuts and antique lace into her designs for her label 'something old… something new'. Her ring master's jacket, a recycled item from the wardrobe of a school with military connections, was made as an entry to the Hand and Lock prize, which encourages the use of embroidery in fashion and textiles. It was mostly inspired by old images of 1930s circus acts and in particular tattooed ladies. The dress, which is just visible under the bright red jacket, was meant to look like a 'showgirl dress' and the jacket like the ringmaster's, slightly too oversized on her, as if she'd just borrowed it.

The back recycles a hand-knitted mohair jumper from the 1980s, which has been felted and worked into with some hand beading. The border is made up of many fabric scraps including silk, tweed and vintage florals all applied by hand with a beaded border and old beads, buttons and brooches added for extra embellishment. The jacket also includes a patchwork panel of cigarette silks sourced from a vintage shop.

LEFT: Jan Knibbs. *Travelling Circus*, 2007.
BELOW: *Travelling Circus*, pocket detail.

WORN

Julia Triston

Julia Triston does not use jackets as a canvas on which to collage, but reconstructs garments from previously worn clothes. She deconstructs each jacket section by section, sometimes right back to its joins, seams and 'landmarks'. New forms are then rebuilt around these frameworks by attaching, inserting and piecing fragments and details, fastenings and features from other garments (which often bear the mark of previous wearers) into the voids and spaces. Julia's collections investigate her interest in the historical research of undergarments, including splits, voids, lacing, form and structure.

ABOVE: Julia Triston. *Blue Flower Jacket* (from the 'Jackets & Skirts Collection'). Upcycled denim jacket reconstructed with second-hand clothing, repurposed embroidered cloths, eyelets, printed textiles, new and vintage lace.

WORN

LEFT: Skirt made from unpicked strippy quilt, with tweed panel, patchwork and embellishment.

Quilt garments

- -

Sometimes you might want to make a garment from scratch rather than just finding something to embellish. The starting point for the transformation of old quilts into skirts and other garments started with an image of a quilted petticoat in the Quilters' Guild Collection. The utilitarian Turkey red petticoat was made by Booth and Fox between 1865 and 1880. A little bit more research indicated that these were not uncommon in the nineteenth century in the UK, USA and Europe. Quilted clothing was indeed very fashionable and in the eighteenth century beautiful petticoats were finely quilted in satin and silk. More utilitarian quilted skirts and petticoats were made in rural areas, and along the North East coast of England were worn by fishermen's wives. These were made from heavier wool and woven dark-coloured fabrics. They were designed to be practical and warm. It took a very basic skirt pattern and old quilts calling out to be transformed into something else and a collection of quilt skirts was started.

LEFT: *Found Flowers* skirt made from very worn patchwork quilt, with Turkey red waistband and needlepoint appliqué.

The strippy skirt was made from a thick utilitarian strippy quilt. Unpicking revealed up to seven layers of fabrics had been used and quilted together for warmth. Careful de-structuring of the quilt allowed some of the fabrics to be extracted, leaving a delicate tracery of needle holes where quilting stitches had been used. Small scraps of fabrics were patchworked onto the top layer of the skirt. The dullness of the original quilt was made more precious by the inclusion of a beautiful piece of needlepoint and a piece of Harris Tweed, complete with the iconic orb logo.

If you are using quilts to make into skirts then you may find it almost impossible to get the two layers of back and front under the foot of a domestic sewing machine. If this is the case then you will need to hand sew the side seams together using a robust thread and an overstitch. This means the skirt will not be as durable as a conventional skirt, but it can still be worn or hung on a wall. The *Found Flowers* skirt was made in a similar way. The quilt used in this instance was unusual in being a Turkey red and blue strippy on one side, and patchwork on the other. It was in poor condition so fabrics unpicked from other parts of the quilt had to be patched onto the surface to hold the whole thing together. The Turkey red fabric from the strippy found its way onto the waistband and to tidy up the hem. A pocket was made and attached and again, my old favourite, a piece of needlepoint, was used to create the suggestion of a flowers with long stems.

Zips are inappropriate when using such old quilts and a handmade loop-and-button placket seemed more in keeping with the style.

Hexagon quilts are easy to find because they are often the first project for beginners at patchwork. Many sewers underestimate the time it takes to assemble a hexagon quilt so you can often find unfinished sections second hand and sometimes piles of flowers constructed of six hexagons overstitched round one central one. The flowers were then assembled, perhaps to create a traditional pattern called 'Grandmother's Flower Garden'.

They are constructed from tiny scraps of fabric tacked over papers that have been accurately cut from drawing round a hexagon template. This is sometimes called English patchwork or mosaic patchwork. The skirt pictured below is made from an unusual hexagon quilt. Normally patchwork is done with cotton fabrics or silk but in this case rayons and synthetic fabrics have been used: the colours and some of the prints suggest these were petticoat or chemise scraps. The quilt was in a sorry state, but the back had such a beautiful texture that I have used a piece of this on the front panel of the skirt. The corded detail round the original coverlet has also been used near the top of the skirt with a waistband made from unfinished canvaswork. This skirt is an excellent example of how you can repurpose something that is really disintegrating and give it a new function and life.

LEFT: Skirt made from recycled hexagon coverlet. Both the back and front of the quilt have been used in the construction and the corsage detail made from the leftover scraps is detachable.

WORN

Quilt dress

A white and blue quilt was used to make this dress. Embroidery transfers were used to overprint the quilt surface of the garment. These were once quite common – free with women's and craft magazines. They are essentially a thin piece of paper with a carbon drawing printed onto them. You iron the transfer from the back onto your piece of cloth. This would provide the outline which would then be stitched over using a series of decorative stitches. They were commonly used to provide motifs for handkerchiefs, tray cloths, tablecloths or detailing on a garment. In the case of the dress they have only been used to give surface interest and pick up the blue colour scheme within the quilt.

If you are buying old transfers you need to check that they have not been used before. If they are still shiny then it is likely the ink has not been ironed off. To make your own transfer pattern, see page 94.

ABOVE: Old embroidery transfers.

WORN

RIGHT: Dress made from an old quilt, Suffolk puffs, print and embroidery.

Transfers

The dress on page 93 has also been embroidered in backstitch with a design taken from an old transfer pattern which has been altered, blown up and marked onto the quilt to give an outline to work with. Here is how to make your own transfer pattern:

ABOVE: Stylized flower motifs embroidered in backstitch. They were redrawn from old embroidery transfer designs.

How to transfer a pattern or drawing

- Blow up your pattern or drawing using a photocopier.

- You will use dressmaker's carbon paper to transfer your design. This comes in different colours and it is best to use a colour which is similar to the colour of your stitching. Cut the carbon and design to the same size for ease of use.

- Pin your drawing to the carbon paper so the carbon paper is facing down and your design is facing up.

- Place onto your fabric and pin once more.

- Working on a hard, flat surface, draw through the design using a biro or hard pencil. It is good to test on a similar piece of foundation fabric, particularly if you are using a piece of quilt as a base.

- You may only get a faint line, but this will be enough to guide you through the stitchery.

- An alternative is to use a soluble fabric marker pen to draw your design freehand onto your garment. Because the pen marks can easily be removed with water you can eradicate marks made by mistake.

An old Clothkits pattern for a pinafore dress was used to construct the dress. This pattern was specifically chosen because it had a front yoke for which I utilized a piece of quilt which had an area of interesting ruching, caused by washing at a high temperature. The blanket wadding had shrunk against the cotton top creating what almost looks like pleating. The top of the yoke has been further embellished with Suffolk puffs and a detachable flower.

The gathered circles of fabric, which in the UK are called Suffolk puffs and in the United States yo-yos, are ideal for the surface embellishment of garments. They can be used on blouses and dresses, as brooches and around hems. They have been sewn onto the bodice of the blue transfer dress to create added interest.

How to make a Suffolk puff

The thing to remember about Suffolk puffs is that you need more fabric than you might anticipate. A circle of fabric with a diameter of 15cm (6in) makes a Suffolk puff which is only 5-7.5cm (2-3in) diameter. Use lightweight fabrics which will gather easily.

ABOVE: Suffolk puffs made from unpicked fabric from the original quilt.

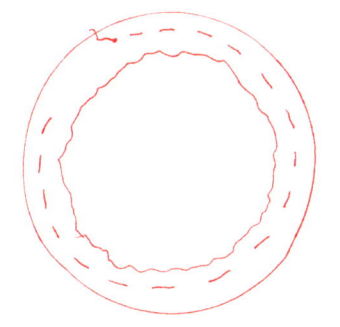

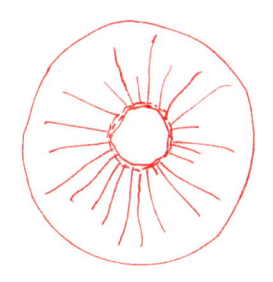

- Draw round a circle template or dish onto fabric and cut out.

- Thread a needle with buttonhole thread, or ordinary sewing thread doubled up, and with a strong knot at the end.

- Sew round the edge of the fabric circle, finger turning as you go and sewing close to the fold. You should use large, even running stitches. Large stitches will result in a small central opening while smaller stitches encourage a large centre opening.

- At the end gather and secure with a strong knot or several overlying stitches.

- Turn inside out and pull into shape.

- Sew onto foundation fabric with small overstitches.

Suffolk puffs can be made in different sizes and you can apply smaller ones on top of bigger ones, or they can be joined together to form a trim.

WORN

Domestic embroidery

Lu Flux

Lu Flux is a British fashion designer who creates unique and charming clothing collections that take inspiration from ideas of British eccentricity. Many of her designs are one-offs because she is using locally sourced materials and has built up relationships with recycling unit staff who put aside materials that they think she can use. Through this connection, she saves fabric going into landfill or being turned into rag waste, and after laundering, is able to transform

ABOVE: Lu Flux. *Arcola Linen Blouse and Florine Patchwork Skirt*. Gee's Bend Collection, 2013.

RIGHT: Lu Flux. *Irby Patchwork Tea Dress*. Gee's Bend Collection, 2013.

WORN

and recycle it into something really special. In the world of fashion she is that rare thing; a sustainable designer. She loves craft and many of the techniques used in the making are labour-intensive and traditional. Embroidery, fabric manipulation and appliqué are used in idiosyncratic ways that make her work unique and outside the 'fast fashion' trade that most of us buy into. Her designs are made to order and so, for example, when she brings patchwork into the garment construction, the garments would be custom-made and she would encourage the client to select, to their taste, from the vast archive of fabric she has collected.

The garments featured in the photograph are influenced by the Gee's Bend quilters of Alabama, who created patchworks far removed from the planned and designed quilts happening elsewhere in the USA. Lu admires the spontaneity of these quilts and hopes to bring this spirit to her own making.

WORN

98

Needlecraft

Lu Flux sometimes uses old embroidered tablecloths in her clothing collections. From the 1920s to the 1950s women's magazines and specialist craft magazines such as *Needlecraft* and *Needlewoman* encouraged women to produce embroidered items for the home. Transfer patterns usually came free with the magazine along with instructions and stitch diagrams and a photograph of the finished product. It could be argued that this type of prescribed needlework kept women firmly in the domestic sphere, making items such as tray cloths, aprons, antimacassars and cushions, which would contribute to an idea of an ideal home. However, it did allow a certain amount of self-expression and certainly encouraged the development of quite sophisticated skills. During the Second World War, the magazines and pattern books moved away from the more decorative and turned to 'Make Do and Mend' features. In the 1950s and early 1960s women were encouraged to embrace the new spirit of design and patterns reflected the emerging graphic styles.

Much of the needlework produced in the home by previous generations of stitchers has fallen out of fashion and can be easily found in charity shops and auctions. Its irrelevance to the way we live today means that, though we can admire the craftwork, we can also cut it up and use it to fashion something new. It is ideal for collaging onto garments.

The petticoat shown left was dip dyed and motifs from domestic embroidery were cut out and appliquéd around the bottom of the skirt. The colour scheme was tightly controlled and only flower embroideries in oranges and yellows were used. In this case the edges of the embroidery were not turned under, and were merely sewn on using a tiny overstitch. You could use this type of domestic embroidery to decorate any garment.

LEFT: Cotton petticoat dip dyed. Collage of flowers cut from domestic embroidery items.

WORN

Smaller projects

If you feel you cannot tackle a major project like collaging onto a garment, there are smaller items that you can make to wear or add interest to clothing. Brooches, hair pieces, collars and bracelets or cuffs can all be easily constructed. **Viv Sliwka** makes her accessories by hand, using time-worn fabrics. She layers up the vintage, hand stitching everything together and often adding embroidered flowers.

Karen Nicol upcycles bags, which she sources at car boot sales and vintage fairs. She has chosen bags made of fabric, so that they can be sewn into easily and once decorated they are given new linings, and sometimes the handles are changed, to bring the vintage a bit more up to date. There is an element of humour in this collection, as each bag has a strap line.

BELOW: Karen Nicol. *Trash Bag*.
OPPOSITE TOP: Viv Sliwka. *Bracelet Cuffs*.

WORN

Ellie Evans

Ellie Evans patchworks together 'pockets', which explore identity and her own family history. She uses these, as well as document holders, as a vehicle to display her findings. These hanging pockets, which refer back to when women used these instead of bags, were very personal spaces for women at a time when they didn't have that much privacy. Originally, anything from love letters to apples could have been kept in them and they were worn close to the body. Ellie's pockets also convey that sense of intimacy with secret compartments and stitched bits in more discreet places. The emotions that rise up as she works through her past are slightly hidden through the construction. Ellie mainly hand stitches, but she also uses digital technology to collage together documents and photographs, which are printed onto fabric. Here we can glimpse bits of text taken from Ellie's primary school reports, mixed in with manipulated photographs of her own favourite clothes. Sometimes she overlays the prints, printing the same piece of fabric twice. There is always some embroidery in Ellie's work and here she has picked out phrases, which have been embroidered in backstitch that she feels are relevant to her character at the time of making. We find she 'doesn't seek centre stage' and is 'only a little reserved in the company of adults'. The pocket in the foreground suggests she is 'small, neat and agile'.

LEFT: Ellie Evans. *Pocket*, 2007. 25 x 18cm (10 x 7in). Digital print and hand stitch.

101

Flower corsage

When I want to work on something a bit smaller I use leftover pieces of vintage quilt to make flower corsages. You may not have access to quilts of this nature so might need to make individual petals from other materials. You could sandwich together old bits of fabric with a bit of blanket in between to create the old quilt look. Use a running stitch or seeding to hold the layers together. At this stage you could even embroider onto the petals or add snippets of lace or motifs from embroidered charity shop finds.

Method

- Lay at least seven petals out in a pleasing arrangement. Do not worry about the raw edges as they add to the charm.

- Using a buttonhole thread or a robust ordinary sewing thread doubled up, sew through the base of the petals with a running stitch. Gather lightly and overlap the bottom of the petals to taste, before finishing off with a good knot or overstitches.

- Cut an appropriate-sized centre and overstitch onto the top of the gathers.

- Collage and couch wispy lengths and scraps of fabric onto the central surface, with some decorative stitches if you wish, and finish with a button, bead or piece of jewellery.

- Cover the back of the corsage with a piece of felt and sew on a brooch back.

ABOVE AND LEFT: Flower corsage constructed from old quilt pieces and old fabrics attached to pieces of blanket with running stitch. Join the components together with a running stitch, which can be lightly gathered.

Going small

Children's and dolls' clothes are particularly poignant as they remind us of our own childhoods. We all have memories of scratchy jumpers, party frocks and our first school uniform. Most of us, of a certain age, did not appreciate the hand-made and longed for shop-bought fashion, but now seek out hand-smocked dresses, Fair Isle knitting and well-worn miniature clothes. I cannot resist tiny garments, and love to embellish them, using them as a base for collaging special little fabric fragments and stitching into them to make them even more special.

The *Ship Boy Jacket* was extremely grubby when I found it and well worn. It was probably a boy's school jacket. I was thinking about how we have dreams when we are children of what we want to do when we grow up, and the piece of found cross stitch on the inside of a sailing ship suggested maybe the owner of this jacket might have had dreams of going to sea. The colour scheme of the cross stitch was brought onto the front of the jacket with the old pieces of patchwork. Cross stitches were used on the lapel to echo the technique hidden on the inside.

The needlepoint poodle used to decorate the little white jacket is a very significant piece of stitching for me as it is one of the first things I remember stitching as a child. We would receive Penelope tapestry kits at Christmas and if we ever finished them they were inserted in a very ugly plastic frame that came with the kit.

If you want to decorate pre-loved children's clothes yourself then be aware that if you plan for a child to actually wear the garment you need to attach all the embellishments firmly. Think carefully about whether the decoration will withstand a modern washing-machine cycle and do not use anything like buttons, which could be a choking hazard, for clothing for very small children.

LEFT: *Poodle Jacket*. Baby's jacket with applied needlepoint, blanket, tweed and wool embroidery.

ABOVE: *Ship Boy Jacket*. Vintage boy's school jacket with cross-stitch panel inserted and patchwork deconstructed from old quilt.

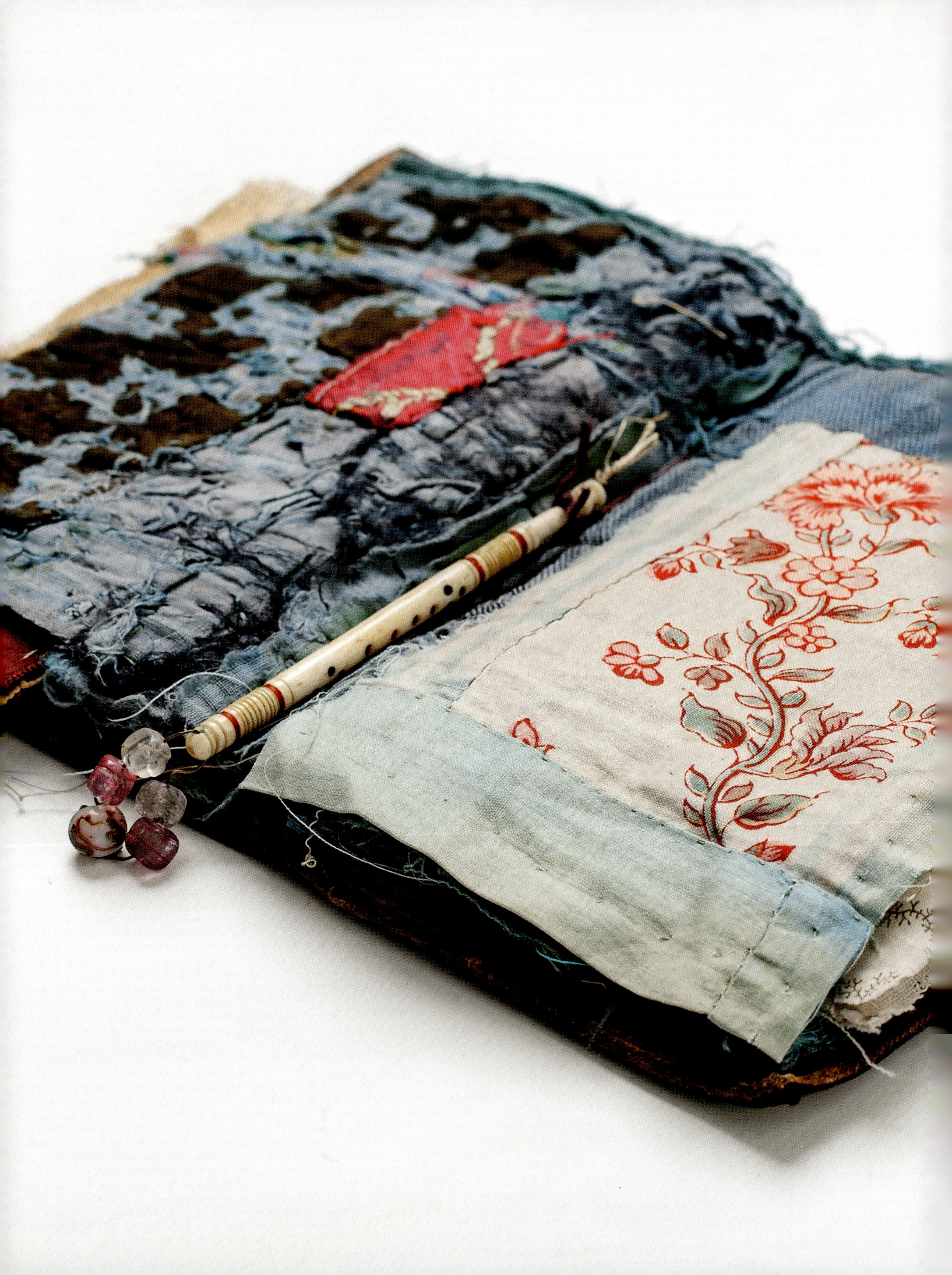

BOOK

For many of us our first experience of holding a book is as a baby when we are given a soft cloth book, which we can chew and stroke. We learn to turn the pages and even as babies we begin to relate to 2D visual imagery and narrative. As a reader my connection with books now is purely through the story, or the information to be gained through reading, but I get a real thrill out of making book forms out of fabric where the tactility of the pages becomes once more intrinsic to the experience and I can create my own picture story through building up the visuals with more cloth. I am trying to recapture the excitement of first handling books and turning the pages to see what the new picture brings.

LEFT: A lace bobbin acts as a bookmark in the centre fold of this fabric book. The cover is a man's leather wallet.

BOOK

Things to consider

There has been a resurgence in the last twenty years of 'Artists' Books', unique and hand-made books, where the cover and contents have been designed to create maximum visual impact. Many of these use extensive mark-making and print-making techniques, layering of paper and fabric plus found printed ephemera and use the full range of mixed-media materials now available to textile artists. In this chapter, however, I am concentrating on book forms that are not journals or sketchbooks, but where the fabric takes priority.

I started making fabric books after seeing the artist Louise Bourgeois's fabric works. Her parents repaired and restored tapestries so she grew up with fabric and tapestries all around her. She used her familiarity with cloth and its handling qualities in her sculpture, using it to create stuffed figures and within garments and installations. She also chose to embroider significant phrases and to create collaged and pieced work within book forms. Holding a needle, sewing and repairing allowed her to work through and 'repair' damage that she suffered as a child, through the breakdown of her parents' relationship. She often used old fabrics that held some resonance for her and in the cloth book *Ode à la Bièvre*, made in 2002, the blue cloth symbolized the importance of the river Bièvre, which ran through her parents' property and was essential to their textile business. Louise continued to make other fabric books such as *Ode à l'oubli*, in which she created 32 fabric collages onto pages made from monogrammed napkins that once belonged in her trousseau.

These books, with their natural cloth pages, side bindings and use of repurposed textiles have influenced me considerably; particularly in the making of my little quilt books.

RIGHT: Ro Bruhn. *Journal*, 2014. 26.5 x 18.5cm (10½ x 7in). Hand-stitched artist's book using leftover furnishing scraps, overdyed fabrics, sari ribbon and silk. This page has been blanket stitched to the page behind. Eventually all the pages are stitched together using pamphlet stitch (see page 118).

BOOK

Size and shape

Large-format books are cumbersome to read and store, and if you are making your pages from fabric rather than paper, they may become quite floppy. Consider making your book quite small. Tiny books immediately convey intimacy and a sense of preciousness. They can be put in a bag and held in the hand.

Look at the books around you. They come in all sorts of sizes and formats, from square to rectangular and in landscape and portrait formats. Your shape might be determined by the type of fabric you have chosen to use; for example, if you are using handkerchiefs or doilies as your pages.

BOOK

Pages

What are your pages going to be made of? Pieces of quilt, blankets, napkins and furnishing fabric are all ideal surfaces onto which to collage and stitch, because they are pretty firm. Your pages may need to be sewn together to cover up the stitching on the back so you need to take this into consideration. If you are using pieces of quilt as your pages, however, it might not be possible to sew them back to back but you might be able to sink the holding and decorative stitches into the top two layers of the quilt without actually going through the back. You need to decide on the number of pages too, as in the end you are going to have to make a workable structure that can be sewn together and which will open flat enough that you can easily see the contents. If you are using numerous pieces of collage, then your book might become quite bulky. I usually make my pages separately and then lay them out on a table when I have finished, to make a final decision about the order. I design the cover last to bring ideas of the colour and content together.

ABOVE RIGHT: Pages ready for assembly. These will be sewn together with a running stitch down the left edge and then a piece of red fabric will be attached around the spine and over the joining stitches with a button detail as in *Thrift Tips*, page 111.

RIGHT: Miloš Tomić. *The Book of Stains, Holes and Patches*. 2007. Pages made from materials found from everywhere; from his grandmother's closet to houses where drunks live. One cannot help but wonder at where these pieces of sometimes dirty and stained textiles have come from and what they have witnessed.

Content

An author has a story to tell or facts to communicate effectively to a reader. A textile artist has rather a different agenda. You may want to convey a message, but it is more likely that your making is connected to aesthetic criteria and that you will make something that pulls materials together that sing for you, and that you want to share that pleasure with a 'reader'. It is useful, however, to think about what your book is about and pull together some sort of theme. It could be:

- A collection of textile samples for a bigger project
- Responses to a particular type of fabric or technique
- The story of a person, place or experience through the use of resonant fabrics
- Colour or texture studies
- A tactile response to a piece of text or a story

My own book forms have often been motivated by the fabrics themselves and a connection to a current body of work, but sometimes also by the need to tell a story. This, after all, is what we expect books to do. You do not want to replicate what real books, made of paper and printed text, do so well, so you need to find a new fabric language to put over your message.

Flowers in the Snow was inspired by a walk through a municipal cemetery in deep snow. The graves were completely obscured and covered in a white blanket, but the vibrant silk and plastic flower heads of weather-resistant floral tributes poked through, reminding us that those underneath were not forgotten. I captured this in some photographs and then mixed these up with verbal tributes collected from gravestone carvings in the same burial ground. I chose to transfer print the photographs onto a pure white damask tablecloth, the flowers slightly obscured by white emulsion and the lettering typed onto the fabric using an old-fashioned typewriter. This technique is described later in this chapter. The book does not have a fabric cover, but is bound into an old springback photograph album.

RIGHT: *Flowers in the Snow*, 2010. Photos transferred onto emulsioned pages and pages gathered into a springback photo album.

BOOK

Jessie Chorley

Jessie Chorley is based in London but grew up in rural Wales and was home schooled by her mother, textile artist Primmy Chorley. Primmy Chorley creates wool-work pictures of her family and significant and celebratory events in their lives such as moving house, the death of a pet, growing things... Some of this has rubbed off on Jessie as, under her mother's tutelage, she became proficient in hand-sewing skills and shares her mother's love of storytelling through stitch.

In her fabric story books, however, she looks outside the home for inspiration and to the magic realism of Angela Carter's writings, particularly *The Magic Toyshop* and *Nights at the Circus*, to inspire her making. She has used old nightwear and silk hankie cases to make the covers and pages of the books. These, once-common items, were often hand quilted to match bedroom sets and came made in subtle pastel colours. Jessie was drawn to the tactile and fragile qualities of the fabrics. Sometimes silk was used with hand-painted detailing and appliqué, and she uses these as a starting point and incorporates these elements into her ongoing stories. She sees the pieces as short stories folding out onto one long page that can be rolled up, but she has also inserted wire so that they can be stood up. Some of the books have separate fabric pages and an image, or just a phrase or word, embroidered in split stitch. Those who have read Angela Carter can see the references to her writings but the words and pictures also allow the 'reader' to conjure up their own imaginary world. Chorley says of these early book forms: 'I was exploring dreams and fragmented memory at the time'.

ABOVE: Jessie Chorley. *Fabric Story Books*, 2004–2010. Hand embroidery, appliqué and found objects inspired by the writing of Angela Carter.

Quilt books

A quilt is a bit like a series of pages. When you partly unpick an old quilt you find the layers of fabric inside tell their own story. My book *Cross Patch* is made entirely from one old utilitarian quilt. The quilt was thick and heavy and unpicking it revealed up to seven layers of fabric interleaved under the quilted strippy top. The pages are thin and made from these 'found' fabrics. The appliquéd St George's crosses have been made with the same materials, carrying the colour across the pages. The whole thing is held together with three buttons, which means the book is easy to pull apart and the order of the pages can be altered. This is a very effective way to pull cloth pages together.

I have often made quilt books at the end of a project where I have pieces left and it is sometimes a way of giving an explanation to the main idea. *Transfer* was pulled together after I had finished my transfer dress (page 93). The quilt I used in the making of the dress was printed with old embroidery transfers, so I have used them creatively within the pages as well as offering a hand-stitched guide on how to use them. A pocket at the back held the original transfers I had used in the project. The pages in this book were bound at the spine with a tight overstitch, and then this was disguised with a piece of fabric that wrapped round the spine and was overstitched into place. *Thrift Tips* was finished in the same way.

BELOW: *Transfer*, 2013. A pocket has been attached to the back page of this book which utilizes old blue embroidery transfers.

TOP: *Thrift Tips*, 2013. A piece of fabric has been pulled round the spine of this book and the pages are attached with the buttons.

RIGHT: *Cross Patch*, 2015. Pages made from an unpicked antique utilitarian quilt.

BOOK

Scroll books

A scroll is usually thought of as a roll of paper that contains text. They could be unrolled so that only a page or part was visible, with the rest of the text rolled to the left and right of the exposed section. Examples have been discovered from thousands of years ago including the Ancient Egyptian and Roman periods. We probably now associate the format of the scroll with the Torah, the most important document of Judaism.

In some cultures scrolls were pictorial. In Japan and China, for example, scrolls held wonderful paintings, often onto silk, which could be rolled-up when not on display. The format of the rolled up story can be a great inspirational starting point for collaged cloth books where only one section might be exposed or there is the opportunity to see the whole piece.

Jan Miller

The flexibility of cloth is used to great effect in Jan Miller's work. Her intimate pieces welcome constant rearrangement and the collaged and narrative elements within the book works change constantly through subtle variations of folding and rolling. Her scroll works can be displayed and seen as flat pieces, but can become 3D forms through the way they are stored, folded or draped. Her work invites the 'reader' to interact with it, to lay it out in new arrangements, turn pages and reconfigure to create new narratives and perspectives.

Jan works with a subtle palette of natural materials, some old, which often contain marks or ghosts from other textile techniques. She will use dyes, painting and screen printing to create deliberate marks, but the inclusion of the accidental fragments and offcuts from these processes adds another echo to the story. Edges are important and usually left raw. Stitches are used thoughtfully to hold the layers in place but are also used as another mark-making tool as they wander across a length of fabric or provide highlights.

Land lines: en bloc is an ongoing project. The nine compartments within the concrete container hold flat, folded and rolled forms interspersed with stones retrieved from local beaches. The stones share the same layered history and provide divisions, which can be altered. Their hard surface provides us with a reminder that the personal narratives held within the soft forms is a changing story as feelings, remembrance of journeys and experience alter with time. Jan is able to edit this library of memories through the removal of an element, a reassessment and readjustment of the surface design and by changing the order. Constant curation by the viewer or the maker offers us new viewpoints each time.

Making a fabric concertina book

OPPOSITE: Jan Miller. *Land lines: en bloc*, 2015. Natural dyes and stains, hand stitch, mixed media.

ABOVE: 'Slitrig binding cloth II' from *Land lines: en bloc*. This piece holds a story of a walk in Hawick from the site of a dye works on the river Slitrig.

Choose a fabric which will hold a crease. Thick linen or calico is ideal or use starch to stiffen a lighter weight fabric.

- Cut your length of fabric. A figure that you can divide easily is ideal. My book is 120 x 14cm (47 x 5½in). This means that I can have 10 pages each 12cm (4¾in) wide.

- Mark the fabric in regular intervals at both top and bottom so you know where to make the folds.

BOOK

- These folds in book making and origami are called mountain and valley folds. If you imagine that your cover will be attached to the back of the first pages of your length of fabric, then your first fold on the left will be a valley fold. This will form your first double-page spread. The mountain folds will be the creases that appear on the edges of the book when it is shut. Make creases through your fabric, ending with a valley fold so that the back cover of the book will be attached behind this final double-page spread.

- Lay out your fabric pieces across the length of the fabric. Be sensitive to the way it will be 'read' and concentrate on getting the layout of the double page spreads right. I have taken strips of fabrics across the folds leading into the next spread but this is a matter of personal choice.

- Attach the fabric with tiny stab stitches. The stitches will show through on the back of the page. Accept this. When you turn the book over you will have inadvertently created a new narrative of stitched sentences.

- The front cover of the book is one piece of fabric, the same size as one of the pages, and I have attached this with tiny stitches. I used a thread the same colour as the page so these stitches are almost invisible. If you do not want your stitches to show at all, glue your cover on with a glue stick.

ABOVE: The simple fabric cover has been sewn on with tiny stab stitches but could have been stuck on with a glue stick.

ABOVE: *Fragments*, 2015. Concertina book with one long collage moving across the pages so the book can be viewed laid out flat or as double-page spreads.

RIGHT: *Fragments* (detail).

BOOK

Wonders with wallets

Men's leather wallets make a wonderful starting point for a book. I choose to repurpose old ones, because the leather has usually become soft through repeated use and the patina of wear and tear fits in with my personal aesthetic. It is even better if you can recycle one from a family member but if you can't you might still be able to imagine who owned it. Sometimes I can make a connection with the previous anonymous owner through stamps or small bits of paper found slipped inside. These pockets are one of the reasons that I choose to use wallets rather than leather book covers, or purses, as they contain potential for further hiding away or inserts.

Don't even think about the pages yet but make your first task gathering together all the bits you want to incorporate in your book. It is essential that you have a colour story to work with. Here I have gathered a variety of green-based collage ingredients together to work with. I need to be willing to cut them up, however precious, and the variety of textures will be stimulating both for me to work with and for the 'reader'. These pieces will form the decoration and pages of the book.

RIGHT: Wallets ready to be made into books, and a colour story emerging through careful selection of fabrics.

115

Cut your pages to this proportion

Fold line

wallet

Method

- Cut out your pages. These are the size of a double-page spread and will eventually be folded and interleaved. They should be about 1cm (⅓in) smaller than the open wallet. I use pieces of thin quilt or coverlet or thick canvas-type cottons or furnishing fabric but you could use any fabric as long as it is robust enough to take the weight of the collage. You could have a mixture of coloured pages or you can keep them uniform. If you are using a thicker fabric, like a bit of quilt, then the wallet may be unable to accommodate more than four pages, however, when you fold them to insert them, these four pages will actually provide 16 surfaces on to which to work.

- Fold your pages and interleave them if you are using a variety of colours so that you can work out the order. Make note of this arrangement, or make a photographic record, so that you can bring them back together in this order when you come to sew the book together at the end.

- Make a tacking stitch down the middle of each open page, so that you know the boundaries of the area you are going to work on.

- Start to lay out and pin your cloth ingredients, creating little collages on each side of the tacked line on both sides of the open page. Regularly return to folding and interleafing so that you can anticipate what it will look like when one arrangement falls next to another.

- When you are happy with the colour and composition, start to sew the pieces on using tiny holding stitches that are barely visible and run round the edge of the cloth holding it down onto the foundation. This might be more familiar to you as a pick stitch, a tailoring term, or a stab stitch. Sometimes I will also use a little overstitch. It is likely that the stitches will show on the other side of the page, but they might be covered up by the collage when you turn the page over to work on the other side. When you come to do the reverse side, you may be able to place the stitches so they sink into the foundation but not all the way through to reveal themselves on the already stitched page.

- You are now ready to add any embroidery to highlight the collage, blend across edges or to create a very definite mark. Again, it is likely that this will come through to the other side, but accept this as an interesting accident. How many of us buy an antique piece and immediately turn it over to look at the stitching on the back? You might like to add further embellishment with buttons, trims or more collage if you feel it needs it.

- When you have finished the appliqué and embroidery fold your pages again and put back in order within the wallet. You will sew the book together with a pamphlet stitch, as described overleaf, which is the simplest way of sewing together several folded pages.

OPPOSITE: These open wallet books demonstrate that what can be seen at the edges and the way the pages overlap each other is part of the story to be told as unexpected layouts emerge.

BOOK

117

BOOK

Pamphlet stitch

- Hold the pages firmly in place with bulldog clips at the top and bottom of each side.

- Along the centre crease of the wallet book, mark three dots at regular intervals with a pencil or an erasable pen. These will be your stitching holes.

- Choose a strong thread to sew your book together. It needs to be something that will go through the eye of the needle and is not so thick that it cannot be pulled through the layers. I tend to use a perle or coton à broder thread. Push the threaded needle through the centre hole (B) and to the outside of the wallet leaving a 7.5cm (3in) tail hanging on the inside of the book.

- Bring the needle back inside the book through the top hole at A and then back out to the spine, through hole C, creating a long stitch down the middle of the book. Bring it back to the middle of the book at B but bringing out the thread on the other side of the long stitch. This gives you two hanging tails, which you can knot together over the long stitch to secure the book.

This method works for larger books too but you will need to make either five or seven holes.

- The inside of the leather wallet will be exposed and you might like to make a further collage, in complementary colours, to stick over these end plates. I stick this, rather than stitching, as leather can be difficult to sew through and you do not want stitches to go through and make an unexpected appearance on the cover of the wallet book. There is, of course, also the potential of inner pockets to insert cloth into or utilize in some way.

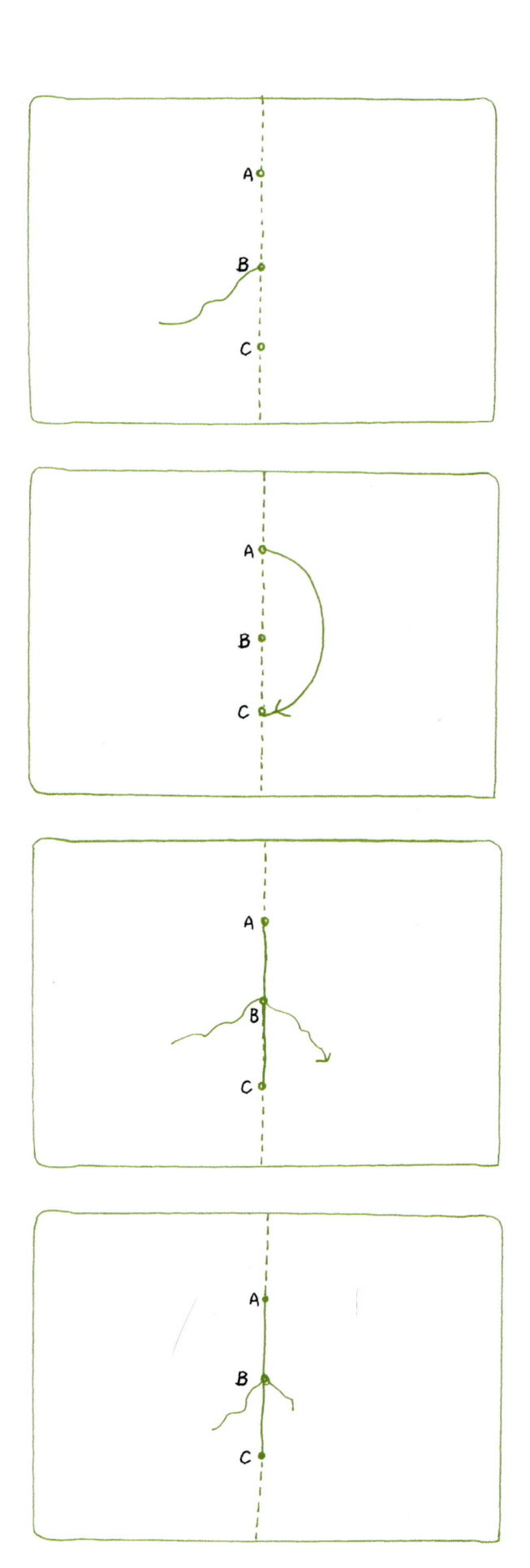

Collections and cloth books

Flower patch

You may wish to use the book format to bring together a collection of samples or a set of techniques. I have done this in *Flower Patch*, collaging straight into a bought sketchbook made of hand-made paper.

My first encounter with embroidery was as a child, seeing my grandmother lovingly stitch floral arrangements, crinoline ladies and gardens onto linen. These were turned into tea cosies, cushions and tablecloths for high tea on Sundays. There seemed to be a real connection between the bright motifs of lupins, daisies and poppies and the beautiful garden she made every year by growing annuals from seed. Some of the pages in this book contain very personal memories. I have included some embroidery done by my grandmother, which, my mother said, was her menopause work. She calmed herself down through stitching a set of beautiful cushions that I can still clearly remember piled upon the sofa. There is much to be learned from this, as I too have found stitching therapeutic at times of stress in my life. Having a piece of sewing to get on with is much better for you than taking a pill.

This type of needlework is no longer relevant to the way we live but rather than keep it folded in a drawer, and if you are brave enough, it can be cut up and collaged into book form and can even be useful as a teaching resource. I taught textiles in an art college for several years and one of the modules I had to teach was hand embroidery. I could distribute a handout with a list of stitches to try and diagrams of how they are worked, but this does not compensate for seeing real stitch examples. In *Flower Patch* you can see much more clearly how a stitch is worked, how its scale can be altered and how it can be mixed with other stitches. Students were encouraged to create designs by closely examining the stitching of a previous generation. I have used a stab stitch to attach the pieces to the page, rather than glue, so they can be removed if I need to incorporate any fragment into another piece of work. The hand-made paper has become almost like cloth through much handling.

ABOVE: *Flower Patch*, 2002. Embroidered motifs from tray cloths, antimacassars and tablecloths sewn into a hand-made paper sketchbook.

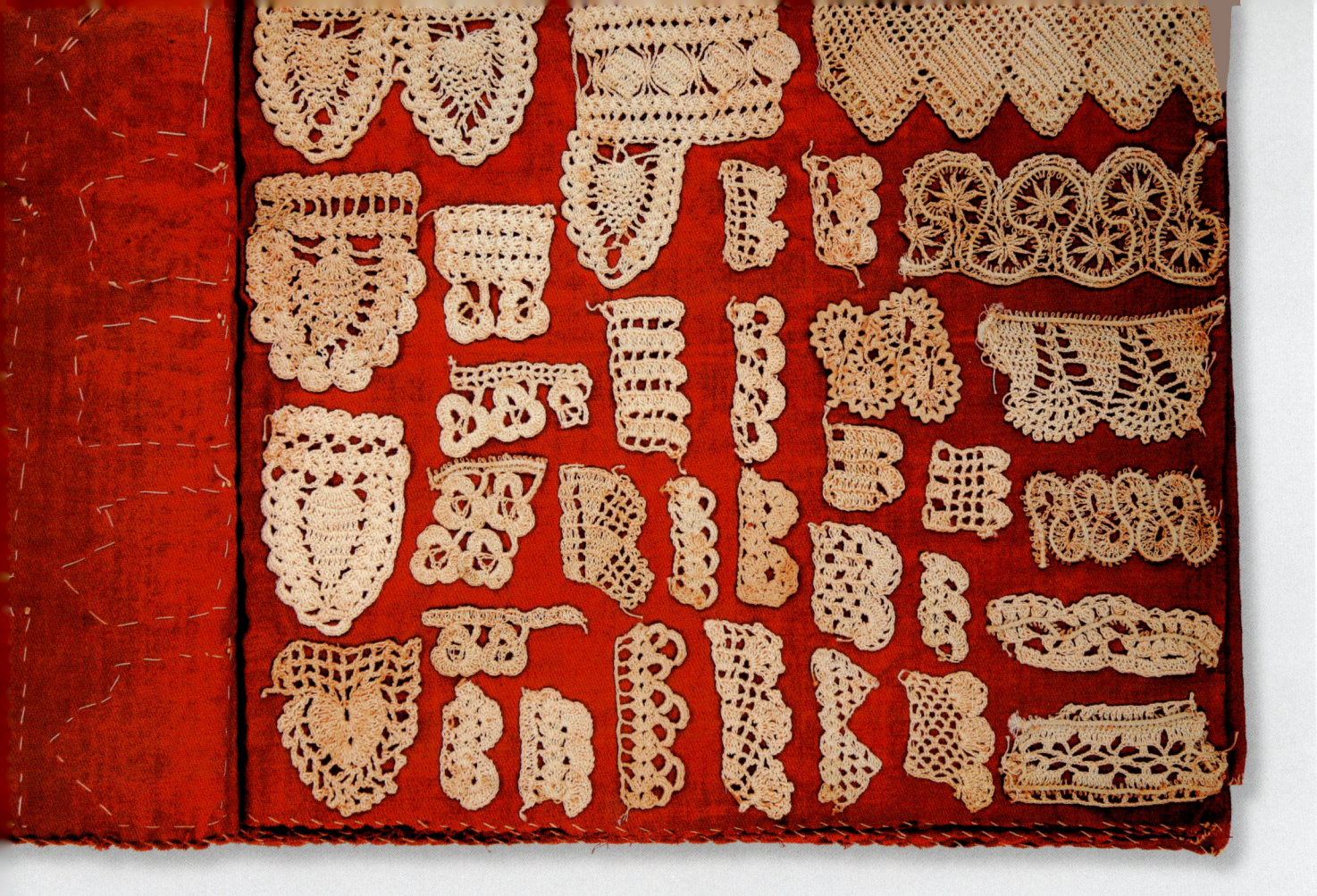

Kaari Meng

Kaari Meng, who runs the wonderful store French General in Los Angeles, travels to France regularly in search of old toile and chintz fabric prints to use as the starting point for designs for the classic French General range of wall coverings. She scours brocantes for old and interesting fabrics. On one such trip she was lucky enough to discover this beautiful red lace sampler book made in 1891 by someone with the initials M.R. It contains samples of bobbin lace, tatting and crochet presumably made by M.R. and carefully stitched onto red pages to maximise the impact. The cream stitches showing through to the other side are almost as beautiful as the samples of lace themselves.

ABOVE AND RIGHT: *M.R. Lace book*, 1891. Sourced in France by Kaari Meng of French General. The cream stitches show through on the back (right).

BOOK

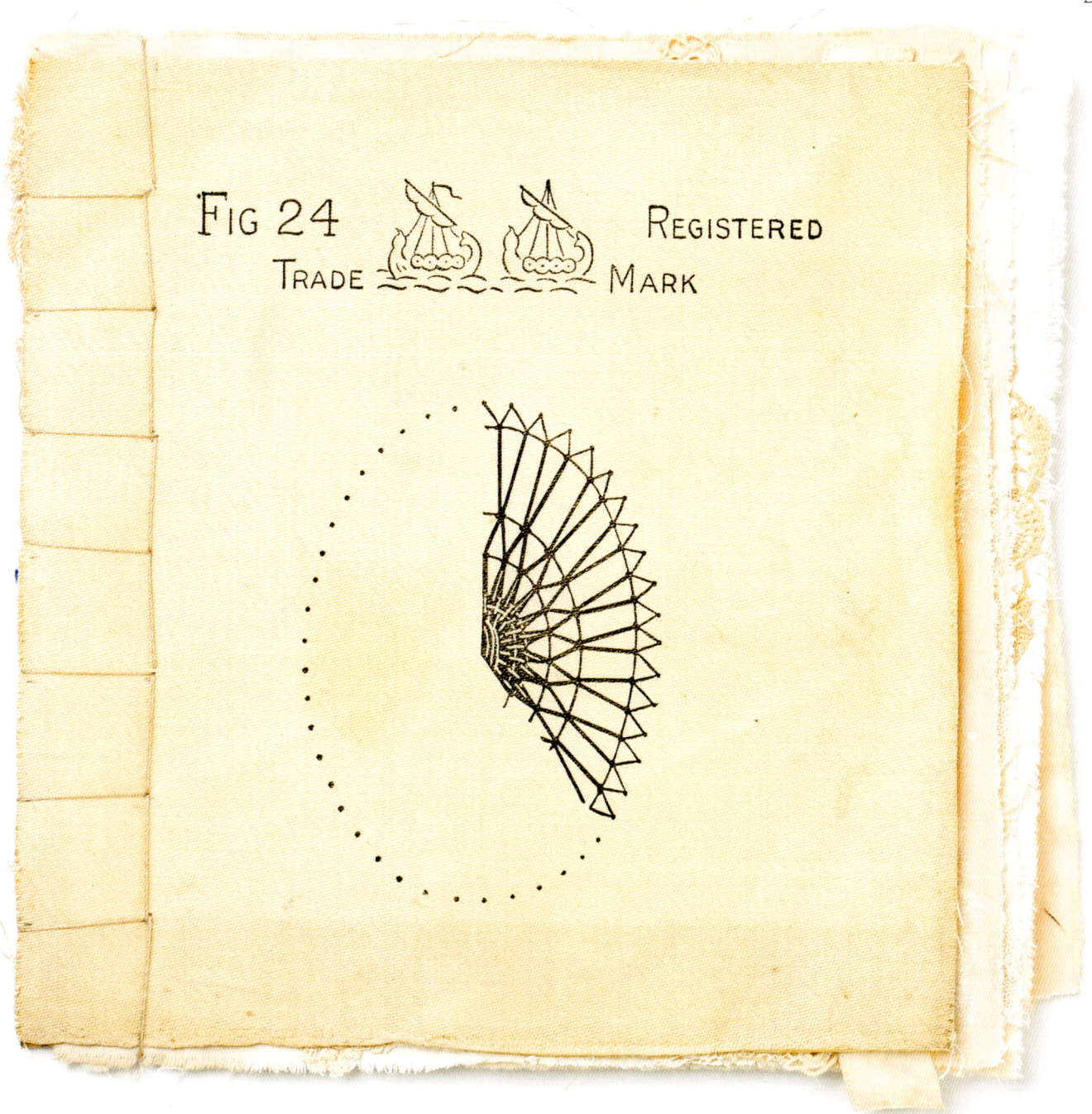

Loving lace

ABOVE: *Fig. 24*, 2015. A 'found' lace pattern cover on this fabric book, which contains painted pages onto which lace scraps and other paper and fabric fragments have been collaged.

In my own lace sample book, *Fig 24*, I too have sewn lace onto fabric pages. These have had surface interest added to them through transferring a fragment of a found drawing, using the method described below, and using a wash of tea and dye over the emulsion paint marks. The book has then been pulled together with a Japanese stab binding. There are many guides to book binding, which will describe this process.

BOOK

Transferring images with emulsion paint

This technique can be less reliable than using commercial transfer papers but you can get really subtle and interesting backgrounds using household emulsion to transfer text or an image onto fabric. Make sure your emulsion is fresh and your brush is not wet as this will dilute the strength of the emulsion.

Ingredients

- White matt emulsion paint
- White or cream fabric – but not a loose weave or embossed or slub surface. An old cotton sheet is ideal.
- Black and white or colour photocopy – Laser and inkjet prints are less effective but experiment until you find what works for you. If you are using words or an image of a place or person you will need to 'flip' on the copier or in an editing programme or they will come out in reverse.
- Wide brush
- Sheet of plastic to protect your table
- Small sponge and bowl of water

Method

- Place a piece of plastic onto a table.

- Place your ironed fabric on the plastic.

- Paint a consistent layer of emulsion onto the part of the fabric where you want to transfer the image. Where the image is going to go must be layered with emulsion but the rest of the fabric could be emulsion free or you could make brush marks elsewhere for added texture.

- Press the photocopy face down in the wet emulsion, making sure there are no wrinkles.

- Allow to dry naturally. Do not dry with a hairdryer or place on a radiator. Let it take its own time and you will have a better transfer.

- Take the sponge, dip it water and wipe over a small area of the back of the paper. Now start to rub away

RIGHT: Detail of a page from *Fig. 24* showing an emulsion transfer onto tea-stained fabric and collage.

122

the paper. Continue to do this until the image is revealed. You may find if you put too much water on or rub too hard the image will come away.

- The fabric surface can be further developed though painting on a solution of tea, for an aged look, or weak commercial fabric dyes or watercolour paint. The emulsion will resist the water-based colour.

I hope the images and examples of book forms described within this chapter will encourage you to experiment with making your own cloth book. The collage will be on a much smaller scale but there are definite challenges to be faced in dealing with the content, colour, order of the pages and the cloth that you choose to make them out of. Think of the pleasure in turning the pages of an illustrated book and try to re-create that through your stitched marks and your careful choice of ingredients.

Conclusion

This book has been written from the perspective of someone who loves to collect, to collage instinctively and to work slowly with hand stitch. I have a reverence for old materials, rescuing them and reinvigorating them, and I hope this book has inspired you to start collecting interesting fabrics and those with a story to tell. You can now develop your own individual approach to textile collage, whether it be making tiny collages, large-scale wall hangings or a portrait, or embellishing a garment with precious detail. I have shown you images by other artists whose work I love and I urge you to keep looking at the work of others, visit galleries and museums, read magazines and books. Do not copy the work of others but close the computer and the book, go to a room of your own and forge ahead with making your own response to the fabrics you have collected and create collages that are unique and personal. I hope you enjoy the process as much as I have.

BELOW: *2 Button Flowers*, 2013. 24 x 24cm (10 x 17in). Covered buttons, needlepoint and stitch onto textile collage.

Artists' websites

Debra Weiss	www.rebebydebraweiss.com
Claire Wellesley-Smith	www.clairewellesleysmith.co.uk
Matthew Harris	www.matthewharriscloth.co.uk
Debbie Lyddon	www.debbielyddon.co.uk
Anne Smith	www.anne-smith.weebly.com
Meta Heemskerk	www.metaheemskerk.com
Claudia Rankin	www.claudiarankin.co.uk
Maria Thomas	www.mariathomastextiles.blogspot.co.uk
Cas Holmes	www.casholmes.textilearts.net
Karen Nicol	www.karennicol.com
Louise Saxton	www.louisesaxton.com
Sue Stone	www.womanwithafish.com
Emily Jo Gibbs	www.emilyjogibbs.co.uk
Louise Baldwin	www.arttextilesmadeinbritain.co.uk
Rosie James	www.rosiejames.com
Jan Knibbs	www.janknibbs.com
Julia Triston	www.juliatriston.com
Lu Flux	www.luflux.com
Viv Sliwka	www.hensteethart.com
Ellie Evans	www.ellie-evans.co.uk
Ro Bruhn	www.robruhn.blogspot.co.uk
Milos Tomic	www.milostomic.com
Jessie Chorley	ww.jessiechorleyinspirations.com
Jan Miller	www.textilestudygroup.co.uk
Kaari Meng	www.frenchgeneral.com

Author websites www.mandypattullo.co.uk
www.threadandthrift.blogspot.co.uk

Suppliers

Jen Jones Welsh Quilts & Blankets
Antique quilts and patchwork
www.jen-jones.com

The Cloth House
Beautiful fabrics from around the world
www.clothhouse.com

The Textile Society
Two antique and textile fairs a year where you can buy unusual antique and ethnic materials
www.textilesociety.org.uk

Dylon
Dyes and advice on dyeing
www.dylon.co.uk

Liberty of London
Iconic printed fabrics
www.liberty.co.uk

French General
Vintage French finds and their own line of patchwork and quilting fabrics inspired by antique French documents
www.frenchgeneral.com

Starched and Crumpled
Antique and vintage linen, textiles and haberdashery
www.starchedandcrumpled.com

Euro Japan Links
Their country cotton range reproduces the look of old Japanese cottons. You can get many colours of sashiko thread from them too
www.eurojapanlinks.com

Empress Mills
Great for all sorts of threads
www.empressmills.co.uk

W.H. Smith
Image-transfer paper
www.whsmith.co.uk

Ebay
Vintage quilts and garments
www.ebay.co.uk

Further reading

Allan, Rosemary E. *North Country Quilts and Coverlets from Beamish Museum*. Beamish, 1987.

Arnett, William et al. *The Quilts of Gee's Bend*. Tinwood, 2002.

Bolton, Janet. *Fabric Pictures*. Jacqui Small, 2015.

Celant, Germano. *Louise Bourgeois The Fabric Works*. Skira, 2010.

Crabtree, Caroline and Christine Shaw. *Quilting, Patchwork and Applique: A World Guide*. Thames and Hudson, 2007.

Golden, Alisa. *Creating Handmade Books*. Sterling, 1998.

Guild, Tricia. *Colour Deconstructed*. Quadrille, 2013.

Harding, Deborah. *Red & White; American Redwork Quilts*. Rizzoli, 2000.

Holmes, Cas. *Stitch Stories*. Batsford, 2015.

Howard, Constance. *The Constance Howard Book of Stitches*. Batsford, 1979.

Koide, Yukiko and Tsuziki, Kyoichi. *Boro: Rags and Tatters from the Far North of Japan*. Aspect Corp, 2009.

Meilach, Dona and Ten Hoor, Elvie. *Collage and Found Art*. Studio Vista, 1965.

Nicol, Karen. *Embellished: New Vintage*. A&C Black 2012.

Oki, Junko. *Punk*. Bungeishunju, 2014.

Prichard, Sue (Ed.). *Quilts 1700–2010 Hidden Histories, Untold Stories*. V&A Publishing, 2012.

Wellesley-Smith, Claire. *Slow Stitch: Mindful and Contemplative Textile Art*. Batsford, 2015.

BELOW: Scraps of needlepoint and wool embroidery embellish the *Found Flowers* quilt skirt.

Index

A
Animals 58-67
Artists' books 106
Audobon, James 60, 69

B
Bags 100-101
Baldwin, Louise 79
Bewick, Thomas 60, 69
Birds 68-69
Blake, Peter 6
Blankets 18
Bondaweb 72, 74
Books, fabric 105-123
Boro 15
Bourgeois, Louise 106
Broderie perse 50
Bruhn, Ro 106-107
Buffon, Comte de, George-Louis Leclerc 60
Bump curtain lining 14

C
Care of fabrics 25
Children's clothes 83, 103
Chorley, Jessie 110
Clothes 81-103
Colour 28
Composition 32
Concertina books 113-114
Content, fabric books 109
Cornell, Joseph 6
Corsage, flower 102
Curtain fabric 14

D
Denim 15
Designers Guild 28
Dress, quilt 92-93
Dyeing 22-23

E
Eiderdowns 12
Embroidery 16, 20, 36, 38, 96-97, 99
Emulsion paint transfer 122-123
Enchanted Forest 58
Evans, Ellie 101

F
Fabric archaeology 21
Fabric collage *see* Textile collage
Fabric collecting 10
Feed sacks 19
Finishing off 39, 64
Flour sacks 19
Flower corsage 102
Flux, Lu 96-97
Framing 41
French General 14, 120

G
Garments 81-103
Gee's Bend 15
Gibbs, Emily Jo 78
Gould, John and Elizabeth 70

H
Harding, Angela 58
Harris, Matthew 23
Hearld, Mark 58
Heemskerk, Meta 40
Holmes, Cas 54, 55

I
Image transfer 72, 122-123

J
Jackets 21, 86-89, 103
James, Rosie 78

L
Lace 16, 120-121
Liberty fabric 14
Line 65
Lyddon, Debbie 24

M
Meng, Kaari 120
Miller, Jan 112
Monotype process 60
Morris, William 58
Mounting 40

N
Natural dyeing 22
Needlecraft 99
Needlepoint 18
Nicol, Karen 66-67, 100

P
Pages, fabric books 108
Painting fabric 23-24
Pamphlet stitch 118
Paper 6, 52-54
Patchwork 6, 11, 15, 21, 51-52, 91, 96-97
Petticoats 90, 98
Portraits
 Animals 58-67
 Birds 68-70
 People 71-79
Printed fabrics 14

Q
Quilt books 111
Quilted garments 90-93
Quilts 6, 11, 15, 21, 31, 42

R
Rankin, Claudia 41
Rauschenberg, Robert 6, 31
Ryan, Rob 58

S
Saxton, Louise 70
Schwitters, Kurt 6
Scroll books 112
Seam ripper 21
Silk 17
Skirts 90-91, 96, 98
Sliwka, Viv 100
Smith, Anne 31
Stitches 36, 38, 63
Storage and care 25
Strippy fabric collage 44-45
Stone, Sue 76-77
Suffolk puffs 94-95

T
Tailors' samples 17, 50
Tapestry 18
Tea dyeing 22
Templates 51, 60, 62, 64
Textile collage 27, 72, 74, 75, 114
 Building up 62-63
 Colour 28
 Composition 32
 Finishing off 39, 64
 Garments 84
 Hunting and gathering 10
 Putting it together 34-35
 Scale 42
 Things to consider 35
Thomas, Maria 53
Threads 20
Tomić, Miloš 108
Transfer monotype 60
Transferring images 72, 122-123
Transfers, embroidery 94
Triston, Julia 83, 89
Turkey Red 12
Tweed 17, 86-87

U
Unpicking 21

W
Wallet books 115-118
Washing fabrics 25
Weiss, Debra 17, 33
Wellesley-Smith, Claire 22
Wool fabrics 17, 25

Picture credits

All images by Michael Wicks except for the following: Mandy Pattullo: pages 32, 112, 113. Alun Callender: page 5, 6 and 7. David Studaris: pages 17 and 33. Claire Wellesley Smith: page 22 (left). Peter Stone: page 23. Debbie Lyddon: page 24. Chris Wilson: page 31. Meta Heemskerk: page 40. Duncan McQueen: page 41. Maria Thomas: page 53. Cas Holmes: page 54. Karen Nicol: pages 66, 67 and 100. Gavin Hansford: page 70. Sue Stone: pages 76 and 77. Lol Johnson: pages 78. Rosie James: page 79 (left); Art Van Go: page 79 (right). Simon Walden: page 88 (left). Jan Knibbs: page 88 (right). Julia Triston: page 89. James Champion: pages 96 and 97. Viv Sliwka : page 101 (top). Ellie Evans : page 101 (bottom). Steve Bruhn: page 106. Miloš Tomić: page 108 (right). Jessie Chorley: page 110. French General: page 120.

Acknowledgements

Thank you to all the artists who have contributed images and information to this book. The book has been enriched through your generosity.

Thank you also to the team at Batsford, and photographer Michael Wicks, for helping me to bring this book to such a colourful and well-designed conclusion.

Lastly, this book would not have been possible without the support of my husband Andrew Pattullo who has encouraged me for the last 40 years to keep stitching and pursue my dreams.